MOVIE ★ ICONS

DE NIRO

EDITOR
PAUL DUNCAN

TEXT
JAMES URSINI

PHOTOS
THE KOBAL COLLECTION

TASCHEN

HONG KONG KÖLN LONDON LOS ANGELES MADRID PARIS TOKYO

ROBERT DE NIRO: EXISTENTIAL MAN

BY JAMES URSINI

ROBERT DE NIRO: DER EXISTENZIALIST

ROBERT DE NIRO: L'EXISTENTIALISTE

ROBERT DE NIRO: EXISTENTIAL MAN

by James Ursini

Most moviegoers associate actor Robert De Niro with adjectives like *intense*, *violent*, *streetwise*, and *brooding*. It is an image that De Niro has carefully nurtured over the last 50 years of his career. Although De Niro was raised by bohemian, artistic parents in largely middle-class surroundings, he identified early on with the youth gangs of New York City's "mean streets" (the setting for his first directorial effort, *A Bronx Tale*). For De Niro these groups of "street toughs" symbolized the rage and disaffection that came to fruition during his teenage years, a disaffection rooted in familial discord—his homosexual father and intellectually distant mother separated when he was six.

Drawing upon his alienation, the young De Niro channeled his energy and enrolled in acting school. There he found an outlet for expressing the emotions he most often repressed around others, projecting them instead into his creations. He learned how to use gesture, voice, and, most importantly, his mesmerizing eyes to convey to the audience the disturbing emotions with which he imbued his characters, from his earliest films like *Mean Streets* (1973, directed by his brother in alienation and lifelong collaborator—Martin Scorsese) through classic portraits of violent, disaffected men like Travis Bickle in *Taxi Driver* (1976) and Jake La Motta in *Raging Bull* (1980) up to and including comic tours de force like the maniacal father in *Meet the Parents* (2000). "One of the things about acting is it allows you to live other people's lives without having to pay the price."

De Niro's style of acting was built upon the foundations laid by earlier cinematic proponents of "the method" (he studied both with Stella Adler and at the Strasberg Studio) like Marlon Brando and James Dean. He fully inhabited the roles he chose, exploring the emotional angst of the characters, not through histrionics but by subtle use of his "instrument." "It's important not to indicate. People don't try to show their feelings, they try to hide them."

**PORTRAIT FOR
'MAD DOG AND GLORY' (1993)**

"There's nothing more contradictory or ironic than life itself."
Robert De Niro

De Niro's legendary disdain for publicity and his guarded nature also suggest a man like many of his characters who chooses to hide his true nature and to veil the emotions that drive him. In *Taxi Driver* he floats in his cab through the "scum-soaked" streets of 1970s New York City, disguising his disgust and outrage, which is finally released in the climactic "holocaust." In *Raging Bull* his brutal bouts in the ring parallel his angst-filled struggles with his family and within himself. In *Awakenings* (1990) he plays a character who has buried his personality and feelings so completely that he becomes catatonic.

Even though De Niro's angst continues to color his choice of roles, even in his more forgettable ones, time and experience have mellowed him. As a positive side effect, De Niro has revealed a more political and socially relevant side, largely rooted in his parents' left-wing sympathies. De Niro has become a force in revitalizing the Tribeca area of New York City, basing his film company and sponsoring a prestigious film festival there. It is as if the actor has finally found a deeper meaning in life back on those now not-so-"mean" streets of his beloved city. "There is no place like New York. It's the most exciting city in the world ... That's the way it is. That's it."

De Niro hosted and appeared in the Naudet-Hanlon documentary on 9/11, which featured the harrowing experiences of firefighters at ground zero. He has also become more involved in Democratic Party politics in the last few elections. And his most recent directorial effort, *The Good Shepherd* (2006), reflects this new activism in its critique of the CIA.

De Niro's journey from alienated teen through conflicted stardom and finally to committed activist again replicates the trajectory of many of his characters, who also travel from the depths of despair to some form of redemption, no matter how unconventional. For, in De Niro's world, art and reality are often indistinguishable.

ENDPAPERS/VOR- UND NACHSATZBLÄTTER/
PAGES DE GARDE
STILLS FROM 'TAXI DRIVER' (1976)

PAGES 2/3
STILL FROM 'CAPE FEAR' (1991)

PAGE 4
STILL FROM 'RAGING BULL' (1980)

PAGES 6/7
**ON THE SET OF 'THE GOOD SHEPHERD'
(2006)**

PAGE 8
**PORTRAIT FOR 'THE GODFATHER: PART II'
(1974)**

OPPOSITE/RECHTS/CI-CONTRE
PORTRAIT FOR 'FRANKENSTEIN' (1994)

ROBERT DE NIRO: DER EXISTENZIALIST

von James Ursini

Die meisten Kinobesucher assoziieren den Schauspieler Robert De Niro mit Eigenschaften wie *eindringlich, brutal, gewieft* und *grüblerisch*. Dies ist ein Image, das De Niro während der letzten 50 Jahre seiner Karriere sorgsam aufgebaut hat. Obwohl De Niro von seinen unkonventionellen Eltern, einem Künstlerehepaar, in einem weitgehend bürgerlichen Umfeld erzogen wurde, identifizierte er sich schon früh mit den Jugendbanden der „mean streets" – der „schäbigen Straßen" – von New York City, in denen auch sein Regiedebüt *In den Straßen der Bronx* angesiedelt ist. Für De Niro symbolisierten jene abgebrühten Gauner die Wut und die Unzufriedenheit, die sich auch bei ihm als Teenager einstellten, bedingt durch den Unfrieden in der eigenen Familie: Sein homosexueller Vater und seine geistig abgehobene Mutter trennten sich, als er sechs Jahre alt war.

Auf der Grundlage seiner eigenen Entfremdung kanalisierte der junge De Niro seine Energie und schrieb sich an der Schauspielschule ein. Dort fand er ein Ventil, um jenen Gefühlen Ausdruck zu verleihen, die er in Gegenwart anderer oft unterdrückte: Er konnte sie stattdessen in seine Figuren hineinprojizieren. Er lernte, wie er Gestik, Stimme und vor allem seine hypnotisierenden Augen einsetzen konnte, um dem Publikum die verstörenden Emotionen zu vermitteln, mit denen er seine Charaktere ausstattete – von seinen frühesten Filmen wie *Hexenkessel* (1973, unter der Regie seines gleichermaßen entfremdeten „Bruders im Geiste" und lebenslangen beruflichen Partners Martin Scorsese) über die klassischen Darstellungen gewalttätiger, desillusionierter Männer wie Travis Bickle in *Taxi Driver* (1976) und Jake La Motta in *Wie ein wilder Stier* (1980) bis hin zu seinen komödiantischen Glanzleistungen wie dem durchgedrehten Vater in *Meine Braut, ihr Vater und ich* (2000). „Die Sache beim Schauspielen ist, dass es einem die Möglichkeit gibt, das Leben anderer Leute zu leben, ohne dass man den Preis dafür zahlen muss."

STILL FROM 'BLOODY MAMA' (1970)
De Niro plays Lloyd Barker, part of the quasi-incestuous Barker clan, led by longtime friend Shelley Winters as Ma. / De Niro spielt Lloyd Barker, ein Mitglied des quasiinzestuösen Barker-Clans, angeführt von Ma, die von Shelley Winters gespielt wird, einer langjährigen Freundin. / Relation quasi incestueuse entre Lloyd Barker (De Niro) et Ma, chef du clan Barker, interprétée par une amie de longue date, Shelley Winters.

„Es gibt nichts Widersprüchlicheres oder Ironischeres als das Leben selbst."
Robert De Niro

De Niros Schauspielstil baute auf den Grundlagen auf, die frühere Vertreter des Method-Acting (er hatte bei Stella Adler und im Strasberg-Studio Unterricht genommen) wie Marlon Brando und James Dean gelegt hatten. Er ging ganz und gar in den Rollen auf, die er wählte, drang in die Angstzustände der Charaktere ein – aber nicht durch theatralisches Getue, sondern durch den geschickten Einsatz seines „Instrumentariums".

De Niros legendäre Publicityscheu und seine zurückhaltende Art lassen einen Mann vermuten, der – wie viele seiner Charaktere – sein wahres Wesen und die Gefühle, die ihn antreiben, lieber verbirgt. In *Taxi Driver* schwimmt er in seinem Taxi durch die „mit Abschaum durchtränkten" New Yorker Straßen der Siebzigerjahre, überspielt seinen Ekel und seine Empörung, bis sie sich in der abschließenden Katastrophe des Films schließlich entladen. In *Wie ein wilder Stier* spiegeln seine brutalen Kämpfe im Ring die von Existenzangst geprägten Auseinandersetzungen mit seiner Familie und mit sich selbst. In *Zeit des Erwachens* (1990) spielt er eine Figur, die ihre Persönlichkeit und ihre Gefühle so vollständig vergräbt, dass sie ins Koma fällt.

Wenngleich De Niros Existenzängste auch weiterhin die Wahl seiner Rollen – auch jener, die man eher vergessen kann – beeinflussen, haben ihn Zeit und Erfahrung milder gestimmt. Als positive Nebenwirkung zeigt sich De Niro mehr und mehr von seiner politisch und sozial engagierten Seite, die wohl ihre Wurzeln größtenteils in den Sympathien seiner Eltern für die politische Linke hat. De Niro spielt eine wichtige Rolle bei der Wiederbelebung des New Yorker Stadtteils Tribeca, wo er seine Produktionsfirma angesiedelt hat und ein renommiertes Filmfestival fördert. Es scheint, als habe er auf den Straßen seiner geliebten Stadt endlich eine tiefere Bedeutung im Leben gefunden. „Es gibt keinen Ort wie New York. Es ist die aufregendste Stadt der Welt ... So ist es nun mal."

De Niro trat als Präsentator und Kommentator der US-Fernsehfassung des 9/11-Dokumentarfilms auf, den die Naudet-Brüder über die entsetzlichen Erlebnisse der Feuerwehrleute am „Ground Zero" am 11. September 2001 mit James Hanlon gedreht hatten. De Niro hat zudem in den letzten Wahlkämpfen wiederholt für die Demokraten Partei ergriffen. Und seine jüngste Regiearbeit, *Der gute Hirte* (2006), zeugt mit ihrer Kritik an der CIA ebenfalls von seinem neuen Aktivismus.

De Niros Lebensweg vom entfremdeten Teenager über eine konfliktgeladene Berühmtheit bis schließlich zum engagierten Aktivisten zeichnet wieder einmal die Laufbahn vieler seiner Charaktere nach, die ebenfalls aus den Abgründen der Verzweiflung aufsteigen zu einer Art Erlösung, ganz gleich, wie unkonventionell sie auch sein mag. Denn in De Niros Welt sind Kunst und Wirklichkeit oft nicht voneinander zu unterscheiden.

PORTRAIT FOR 'THE GANG THAT COULDN'T SHOOT STRAIGHT' (1971)
A fresh-faced De Niro in a light-hearted performance as Mario. / Ein unverbrauchtes Gesicht in einer fröhlichen Rolle: De Niro als Mario. / Un De Niro au visage juvénile dans une interprétation enjouée du rôle de Mario.

ROBERT DE NIRO : L'EXISTENTIALISTE

James Ursini

Dans l'esprit de la plupart des spectateurs, le nom de Robert De Niro est associé à des qualificatifs comme *entier, violent, malin* et *taciturne*. C'est une image que l'acteur a soigneusement entretenue pendant ses cinquante ans de carrière. Bien qu'il ait grandi dans une famille d'artistes bohème dans un milieu plutôt bourgeois, il s'est identifié très tôt aux bandes de jeunes des bas quartiers de New York (sujet du premier film qu'il a réalisé, *Il était une fois le Bronx*). Pour De Niro, ces bandes de « voyous » symbolisent la colère et le détachement qui ont grandi en lui au cours de son adolescence. Une désaffection née de la discorde familiale, son père, homosexuel, et sa mère, intellectuelle et distante, s'étant séparés lorsqu'il avait six ans.

Puisant dans cette impression de détachement, le jeune De Niro canalise son énergie en s'inscrivant dans une école d'art dramatique. Il découvre là un exutoire aux émotions qu'il réprime généralement en présence d'autrui, préférant les projeter dans son œuvre artistique. Il apprend à utiliser les gestes, la voix et surtout son regard captivant pour transmettre au public les sentiments troubles dont il imprègne ses personnages. C'est le cas dans ses premiers films tels que *Mean Streets* (réalisé en 1973 par Martin Scorsese, son âme sœur et son complice de toujours), dans son interprétation légendaire de personnages violents et décalés comme Travis Bickle dans *Taxi Driver* (1976) ou encore Jake La Motta dans *Raging Bull* (1980), mais également dans ses numéros d'acteur comiques, comme celui du père maniaque de *Mon beau-père et moi* (2000).

PORTRAIT FOR 'MEAN STREETS' (1973)
De Niro's breakthrough role as Johnny Boy in soon-to-be perennial collaborator Martin Scorsese's gritty study of the streets of Little Italy. / De Niros Durchbruch kam mit seiner Rolle als Johnny Boy in dieser unverblümten Studie der Straßen von Little Italy unter der Regie von Martin Scorsese, mit dem er bald ein festes Team bildete. / La révélation avec le rôle de Johnny Boy dans ce tableau réaliste de Little Italy, première d'une longue série de collaborations avec Martin Scorsese.

« Il n'y a rien de plus contradictoire ni d'ironique que la vie elle-même. »
Robert De Niro

«Ce qui est bien dans le métier d'acteur, c'est qu'on peut vivre dans la peau d'un autre sans avoir à en payer le prix.»

Le jeu de Robert De Niro (qui étudie avec Stella Adler et à l'Actors Studio) repose sur les fondations déjà posées par d'autres adeptes de la méthode Stanislavski, comme Marlon Brando et James Dean. Habitant totalement les rôles qu'il choisit, il explore les angoisses et les émotions des personnages non par un jeu théâtral, mais par l'utilisation subtile de son «instrument». «Il ne faut pas être démonstratif. Les gens n'essaient pas de montrer leurs sentiments, ils tentent au contraire de les cacher.»

Son légendaire dédain pour l'exposition médiatique et son naturel réservé laissent deviner un homme semblable à nombre de ses personnages, qui s'efforce de masquer sa vraie nature et de voiler les émotions qui l'animent. Dans *Taxi Driver*, il sillonne les rues «infestées de vermine» du New York des années 1970, dissimulant le dégoût et l'indignation qu'il ne libérera que lors de l'«holocauste» final. Dans *Raging Bull*, ses combats brutaux sur le ring font écho à ses conflits familiaux et à ses luttes internes. Dans *L'Éveil* (1990), son personnage a si bien étouffé ses sentiments et sa personnalité qu'il en devient catatonique.

Bien que l'angoisse existentielle de Robert De Niro continue de déteindre sur le choix de ses personnages, même les moins marquants, le temps et l'expérience l'ont quelque peu adouci. Cela a eu pour effet positif de révéler chez lui une sensibilité politique et sociale largement héritée de ses parents de gauche. De Niro a contribué à la revitalisation du quartier new-yorkais de Tribeca, où il a implanté sa société de production et parrainé un prestigieux festival de cinéma. L'acteur semble avoir enfin trouvé un sens à sa vie dans les rues autrefois si sordides de sa ville natale. «Rien ne vaut New York. C'est la ville la plus excitante au monde... C'est comme ça. On n'y peut rien.»

De Niro apparaît dans le documentaire *11/09, New York 11 septembre* de Naudet-Hanlon, qui témoigne de la tragique expérience des combattants du feu au pied des Twin Towers. Il s'est également engagé auprès du Parti démocrate au cours des trois dernières élections présidentielles. Et le dernier film qu'il a réalisé, *Raisons d'État* (2006), reflète son nouveau militantisme par sa critique acerbe de la CIA.

D'abord adolescent rebelle, puis star torturée et enfin militant engagé, De Niro a suivi la même trajectoire que nombre de ses personnages, qui évoluent des tréfonds du désespoir jusqu'à une forme de rédemption, aussi peu conventionnelle soit-elle. Car dans l'univers de Robert De Niro, l'art et la réalité sont souvent indissociables.

STILL FROM 'FALLING IN LOVE' (1984)
Two modern screen legends together in a minor film: Meryl Streep and De Niro. / Zwei Leinwandlegenden unserer Tage in einem kleinen Film: Meryl Streep und De Niro. / Deux légendes du cinéma moderne dans un film mineur: Meryl Streep et De Niro.

PAGE 22
PORTRAIT

2
VISUAL FILMOGRAPHY

FILMOGRAFIE IN BILDERN

FILMOGRAPHIE EN IMAGES

STILL FROM 'GREETINGS' (1968)
A quintessential 1960s satire. Jon Rubin (De Niro) learns about Peeping Toms and tries to avoid the draft. / Eine typische Satire der 1960er-Jahre. Jon Rubin (De Niro) liest von Spannern und versucht, sich vor dem Wehrdienst zu drücken. / Jon Rubin (De Niro) découvre le voyeurisme et tente d'échapper à la conscription dans cette satire typique des années 1960.

"I didn't have a problem with rejection, because when you go into an audition, you're rejected already. There are hundreds of other actors. You're behind the eight ball when you go in there."
Robert De Niro

„Ich hatte kein Problem damit, abgelehnt zu werden, denn wenn man zum Vorsprechen geht, dann wurde man ja bereits abgelehnt. Es gibt Hunderte anderer Schauspieler. Du steckst in der Klemme, wenn du da reingehst."
Robert De Niro

POSTER FOR 'GREETINGS' (1968)
This poster illustrates the scene where Jon Rubin persuades a girl to undress under the pretext that he is making an art film. / Dieses Plakat illustriert jene Szene, in der Jon Rubin ein Mädchen unter dem Vorwand, einen Essayfilm mit ihr zu drehen, überredet, sich zu entkleiden. / Cette affiche illustre la scène où Jon Rubin convainc une jeune femme de se dévêtir au prétexte qu'il est en train de tourner un film artistique.

« Je ne craignais pas d'être rejeté, car quand on passe une audition, on est rejeté d'emblée. Il y a des centaines d'autres acteurs. Quand on arrive là-dedans, on est moins que rien. »
Robert De Niro

STILL FROM 'BLOODY MAMA' (1970)
Director Roger Corman plays up the psychosexual
dimensions of Ma Barker and her wayward sons.
De Niro is in the bathtub. / Regisseur Roger Corman
hebt die psychosexuelle Dimension von Ma Barker und
ihren missratenen Söhnen hervor. De Niro sitzt hier im
Waschzuber. / Le réalisateur Roger Corman souligne les
relations troubles de Ma Barker et de ses vauriens de
fils, dont Lloyd (De Niro) dans la bassine.

"He was skinny and very gentle,
with dark gentle eyes."
Shelley Winters, actress

„Er war dürr und sehr sanft,
mit dunklen, sanften Augen."
Shelley Winters, Schauspielerin

« Il était gentil et maigrichon,
avec des yeux noirs et doux. »
Shelley Winters, actrice

STILL FROM 'BLOODY MAMA' (1970)
Ma (Shelley Winters) shifts mood from tyrannical to
compassionate, cookies and all, as she comforts her
drug-addicted son Lloyd (De Niro). / Die Launen von
Ma (Shelley Winters) wechseln zwischen Tyrannei und
Mitgefühl und kreisen um Kekse und alles mögliche
andere, als sie ihren drogensüchtigen Sohn Lloyd
(De Niro) tröstet. / Ma (Shelley Winters) passe de
la tyrannie à la compassion (et aux cookies) pour
réconforter Lloyd, son fils toxicomane.

**PORTRAIT FOR 'THE GANG THAT COULDN'T
SHOOT STRAIGHT' (1971)**
De Niro shows evidence of the humorous side of his
acting style, which will hold him in good stead later in
his career. / De Niro beweist hier bereits die humorvolle
Seite seines Schauspieltalents, die ihm in den späteren
Jahren seiner Karriere noch zugutekommen wird. /
De Niro révèle l'aspect comique de ses talents de
comédien, qui lui sera très utile plus tard dans sa
carrière.

STILLS FROM 'HI, MOM!' (1970)
Brian De Palma's quasi-sequel to 'Greetings.'
Jon Rubin (De Niro) as Peeping Tom, buyer of top-
quality prophylactics, and actor. / Eine Art Fortsetzung
zu Greetings – Grüße von Brian De Palma: Jon Rubin
(De Niro) als Spanner, Käufer hochwertiger Kondome
und Schauspieler. / Dans cette « suite » de Greetings
signée Brian De Palma, Jon Rubin (De Niro) apparaît
en voyeur, en acheteur de préservatifs et en
comédien amateur.

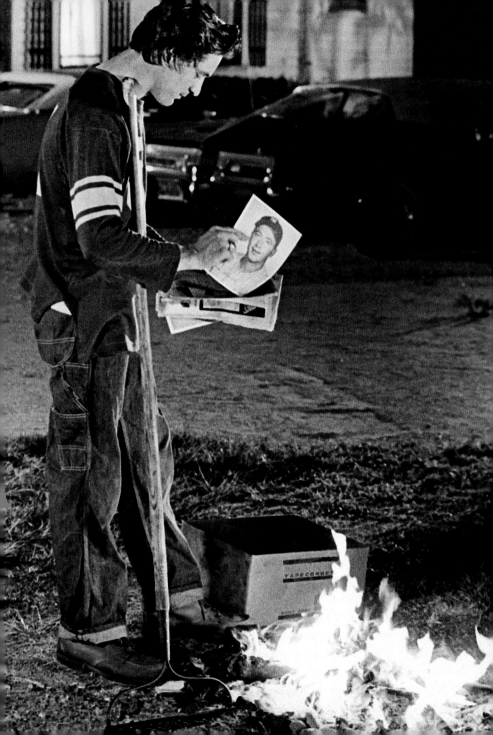

**STILL FROM 'BANG THE DRUM SLOWLY'
(1973)**
De Niro's research included three weeks in Georgia
to get the accent and finding out how baseball players
sat and relaxed in the dugout during the games. / Zur
Vorbereitung auf den Film verbrachte De Niro drei
Wochen in Georgia, um den Südstaatenakzent zu lernen
und herauszufinden, wie Baseballspieler während des
Spiels auf der Bank saßen und sich entspannten. / Pour
se préparer, De Niro passe trois semaines en Géorgie
pour apprendre l'accent et étudie la façon dont les
joueurs se détendent sur le banc de touche pendant
les matchs.

**STILL FROM 'BANG THE DRUM SLOWLY'
(1973)**
Critics raved over De Niro's portrayal of the terminally
ill baseball player Bruce Pearson. / Die Kritiker waren
begeistert von De Niros Darstellung des todkranken
Baseballspielers Bruce Pearson. / La critique s'extasie
sur son interprétation du personnage de Bruce Pearson,
joueur de base-ball atteint d'une maladie incurable.

STILL FROM 'MEAN STREETS' (1973)
As Johnny Boy, De Niro projects the manic energy
of the unpredictable street kid. The actors improvised
scenes and Scorsese rewrote before filming. / Als
Johnny Boy verkörpert De Niro die manische Energie
eines Straßenjungen. Die Darsteller improvisierten
streckenweise, und Scorsese schrieb kurz vor dem Dreh
noch Szenen um. / De Niro, alias Johnny Boy, possède
l'énergie incontrôlable du gamin des rues. Face aux
improvisations des acteurs, Scorsese réécrit les scènes
avant le tournage.

*"We were both brought up in the same area and
we see things the same way. I think also we both
had the sense of being outsiders."*
Martin Scorsese, director

*„Wir wuchsen beide in der gleichen Gegend auf,
und wir sehen Dinge auf die gleiche Weise. Ich
denke auch, dass wir beide das Gefühl hatten,
Außenseiter zu sein."*
Martin Scorsese, Regisseur

*« Nous avons grandi au même endroit et nous
voyons les choses de la même manière. Je crois
aussi que nous avions tous les deux le sentiment
d'être des exclus. »*
Martin Scorsese, réalisateur

STILL FROM 'MEAN STREETS' (1973)
De Niro and guns, soon to be a potent symbol for the
actor in his many violent roles. / De Niro mit einer jener
Schusswaffen, die für den Schauspieler in seinen
zahlreichen gewalttätigen Rollen bald zum Symbol
wurden. / De Niro brandissant l'objet auquel il sera
bientôt associé dans ses nombreux rôles violents.

PAGES 34/35
STILL FROM 'THE GODFATHER: PART II' (1974)
Another gun, this time wrapped in flames, as the young
Godfather secures his own legacy as a don. / Mit einer
weiteren Schusswaffe – diesmal in Flammen – sichert
sich der junge Pate seinen Machtanspruch als
Mafiaboss. / Un autre flingue, enveloppé d'un linge
enflammé : le jeune Parrain réaffirme son statut
légitime de boss de la mafia.

STILL FROM 'THE GODFATHER: PART II' (1974)
The young Vito Corleone as judge and mediator on the
streets of Little Italy. / Der junge Vito Corleone als
Richter und Vermittler in den Straßen von Little Italy. /
Le jeune Vito Corleone, à la fois juge et médiateur dans
les rues de Little Italy.

STILL FROM 'THE GODFATHER: PART II' (1974)
Taking a gesture from Marlon Brando's performance as
the aging Vito Corleone. De Niro also had a dentist fit a
small prosthesis to enlarge his jowls. / Die Geste
übernahm er von Marlon Brando, der den gealterten
Vito Corleone spielte. De Niro ließ zudem von einem
Kieferorthopäden eine kleine Prothese anfertigen, die
seine Backen vergrößerte. / De Niro, qui s'est fait
poser une prothèse pour s'élargir la mâchoire, imite
le geste du Vito Corleone plus âgé interprété par
Marlon Brando.

ON THE SET OF 'THE LAST TYCOON' (1976)
Director Elia Kazan with De Niro and Jeanne Moreau
on the set. / Regisseur Elia Kazan mit De Niro und
Jeanne Moreau bei den Dreharbeiten. / Le réalisateur
Elia Kazan sur le tournage, avec Robert De Niro et
Jeanne Moreau.

STILL FROM 'THE LAST TYCOON' (1976)
Movie mogul Monroe Stahr, based by novelist F. Scott
Fitzgerald on his boss Irving Thalberg, tries to secure
his ideal woman (Ingrid Boulting). / Der Filmmogul
Monroe Stahr, den Romanautor F. Scott Fitzgerald
seinem Boss Irving Thalberg nachempfand, versucht
seine Idealfrau (Ingrid Boulting) festzuhalten. /
Le producteur Monroe Stahr, inspiré d'Irving Thalberg
dans le roman de F. Scott Fitzgerald, tente de retenir
la femme idéale (Ingrid Boulting).

STILL FROM 'TAXI DRIVER' (1976)
In one of the most intense performances of the last
40 years of film history: De Niro as psychopath Travis
Bickle. / Eine der stärksten schauspielerischen
Leistungen der letzten vier Jahrzehnte der Film-
geschichte: De Niro als Psychopath Travis Bickle. /
Dans le rôle du psychopathe Travis Bickle, l'un des
numéros d'acteur les plus saisissants de ces
quarante dernières années.

POSTER ARTWORK FOR 'TAXI DRIVER' (1976)

STILL FROM 'TAXI DRIVER' (1976)
Travis finds a child to rescue in the "savage wilds" of
New York City, teen prostitute Iris (Jodie Foster). /
Travis findet in der minderjährigen Prostituierten Iris
(Jodie Foster) ein Kind, das er in der „Wildnis" von
New York City retten kann. / Dans la jungle urbaine de
New York, Travis trouve une âme à sauver, celle de la
jeune prostituée Iris (Jodie Foster).

STILL FROM 'TAXI DRIVER' (1976)
With a minimum of gesture, De Niro conveys the
alienation and existential despair of "God's lonely man." /
Mit einem Minimum an Gestik vermittelt De Niro die
Entfremdung und Existenzangst von „Gottes
einsamstem Mann". / Avec un minimum de gestes,
De Niro exprime l'aliénation et le désespoir existentiel
de l'« homme solitaire de Dieu ».

STILL FROM 'TAXI DRIVER' (1976)
"Are you talking to me?" The iconic and frightening
mirror scene. / „Redest du mit mir?" Die legendäre
furchterregende Spiegelszene. / « C'est à moi que tu
parles ? » La scène du miroir, légendaire et glaçante.

*"One of the things about acting is it allows you
to live other people's lives without having to pay
the price."*
Robert De Niro

*„Die Sache beim Schauspielen ist, dass es einem
die Möglichkeit gibt, das Leben anderer Leute zu
leben, ohne dass man den Preis dafür zahlen muss."*
Robert De Niro

*« Ce qui est bien dans le métier d'acteur, c'est qu'on
peut vivre dans la peau d'un autre sans avoir à en
payer le prix. »*
Robert De Niro

STILL FROM 'TAXI DRIVER' (1976)
The character's schizophrenia reaches critical mass. /
Die Schizophrenie der Figur hat ihren kritischen Punkt
erreicht. / La schizophrénie du personnage atteint un
point critique.

ON THE SET OF '1900' (1976)
De Niro as the spoiled landowner's son cavorts in this Marxist critique of Italian society. Director Bernardo Bertolucci is in the background to the right of the girl. / De Niro spielt in dieser marxistischen Kritik an der italienischen Gesellschaft einen verwöhnten Gutsherrensohn. Regisseur Bernardo Bertolucci ist im Hintergrund rechts von dem Mädchen zu sehen. / De Niro en fils de riche propriétaire dans une critique marxiste de la société italienne signée Bernardo Bertolucci (à droite derrière la fille).

"It's always difficult to do a love scene in a movie. Everyone is there, they're all watching, and you get very self-conscious."
Robert De Niro

„Es ist immer schwierig, eine Liebesszene in einem Film zu drehen. Alle sind da, schauen zu, und man ist sehr gehemmt."
Robert De Niro

« C'est toujours difficile de tourner une scène d'amour. Tout le monde est là, tout le monde vous regarde, et on se sent très mal à l'aise. »
Robert De Niro

ON THE SET OF '1900' (1976)
Bernardo Bertolucci's (right) authoritarian style
of directing was not sympathetic to De Niro's more
collaborative, improvisational background. / Bernardo
Bertoluccis (rechts) autoritärer Regiestil vertrug sich
nicht gut mit der Spielweise von De Niro, der mehr an
Zusammenarbeit und Improvisation gewöhnt war. /
Le style autoritaire de Bernardo Bertolucci (à droite)
ne convient guère à De Niro, habitué à plus de
collaboration et d'improvisation.

STILL FROM 'NEW YORK, NEW YORK' (1977)
This homage to MGM's classic musicals, many of
which were directed by costar Liza Minnelli's father,
Vincente Minnelli, follows the rise and fall of a singer
and a saxophonist. / Diese Hommage an jene klassischen
Musicals von MGM, bei denen häufig Vincente Minnelli,
der Vater der weiblichen Hauptdarstellerin Liza Minnelli,
Regie geführt hatte, verfolgt den Aufstieg und Fall einer
Sängerin und eines Saxophonisten. / Cet hommage aux
comédies musicales de la MGM, dont beaucoup furent
réalisées par Vincente Minnelli, le père de sa partenaire
Liza Minnelli, retrace l'ascension et la déchéance d'une
chanteuse et d'un saxophoniste.

*"I don't like to watch my own movies—I fall asleep
at my own movies."*
Robert De Niro

*„Ich schaue mir nicht gern meine eigenen Filme
an - ich schlafe bei meinen eigenen Filmen ein."*
Robert De Niro

*« Je n'aime pas regarder mes propres films;
en général, je m'endors. »*
Robert De Niro

STILL FROM 'NEW YORK, NEW YORK' (1977)
The original script was thrown out and plot/dialogue
was improvised, leading to the budget tripling and the
shooting time almost doubling. / Das ursprüngliche
Drehbuch wurde verworfen, und sowohl der
Handlungsablauf als auch die Dialoge wurden
improvisiert, was dazu führte, dass die Dreharbeiten
dreimal so teuer waren und doppelt so lange dauerten
wie veranschlagt. / Le scénario original cède la place à
une intrigue et à des dialogues improvisés, ce qui triple
le budget et double presque le temps de tournage.

*"The hardest thing about being famous is
that people are always nice to you. You're in a
conversation and everybody's agreeing with what
you're saying—even if you say something totally
crazy. You need people who can tell you what you
don't want to hear."*
Robert De Niro

*„Das Härteste am Berühmtsein ist, dass die Leute
immer nett zu einem sind. Man führt ein Gespräch,
und alle stimmen dem zu, was man sagt - selbst
wenn es völlig bekloppt ist. Du brauchst Menschen,
die dir sagen können, was du nicht hören willst."*
Robert De Niro

*« Le plus dur, quand on est célèbre, c'est que tout le
monde est gentil avec vous. Quand vous discutez,
les gens sont toujours d'accord avec vous, même si
vous dites n'importe quoi. On a besoin de gens qui
puissent dire ce qu'on ne veut pas entendre. »*
Robert De Niro

STILL FROM 'NEW YORK, NEW YORK' (1977)
In the end, the film partly becomes a meditation on the
price an obsessive artist pays for his singular focus. /
Am Ende gerät der Film streckenweise zu einer
nachdenklichen Abhandlung über den Preis, den ein
obsessiver Künstler für seine Scheuklappensicht zahlen
muss. / Le film s'interroge sur le prix qu'un artiste
obsessionnel est prêt à payer pour sa passion.

STILL FROM 'THE DEER HUNTER' (1978)
The film, which opens with the wedding of one of the
main characters, follows the lives of a group of steel
workers who go off to fight in Vietnam. / Der Film, der
mit der Hochzeit einer der Hauptfiguren beginnt, folgt
den Erlebnissen einer Gruppe von Stahlarbeitern, die in
den Vietnamkrieg ziehen. / Ce film, qui s'ouvre sur le
mariage d'un des protagonistes, raconte la vie d'un
groupe d'ouvriers sidérurgistes partis faire la guerre au
Vietnam.

*"Robert De Niro is a very intense actor. He doesn't
play joy very well."*
Neil Simon, writer

*„Robert De Niro ist ein sehr konzentrierter
Schauspieler. Freude kann er nicht sehr gut
darstellen."*
Neil Simon, Drehbuchautor

*« Robert De Niro est un acteur très grave.
Il n'exprime pas très bien la joie. »*
Neil Simon, scénariste

STILL FROM 'THE DEER HUNTER' (1978)
The laughter, hijinks, mock fights, and
camaraderie of the group are punctured by an
undercurrent of something dark on the horizon. /
Hinter Ausgelassenheit, albernen Spielchen und
Kameradschaft innerhalb der Gruppe zieht
unterschwellig die Vorahnung einer düsteren
Bedrohung am Horizont auf. / Les pitreries,
les chamailleries et la camaraderie du groupe
sont assombries par une vague menace planant
sur l'horizon.

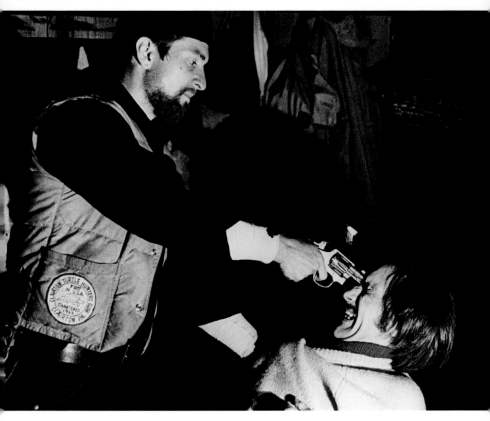

STILL FROM 'THE DEER HUNTER' (1978)
Here Michael (De Niro) shows Stan (John Cazale) the
explosive violence that hides just below the surface
of his character. / Hier gibt Michael (De Niro) Stan
(John Cazale) eine Kostprobe der explosiven Gewalt,
die dicht unter der Oberfläche seines Charakters
lauert. / Michael (De Niro) révèle à Stan (John Cazale)
la violence explosive qui affleure sous sa personnalité
joviale.

"I thought the [Vietnam] war was wrong but what
bothered me was that people who went to war
became victims of it."
Robert De Niro

„Ich fand den [Vietnam-]Krieg falsch, aber was
mich umtrieb, war, dass Leute, die in den Krieg
zogen, dessen Opfer wurden."
Robert De Niro

« J'étais contre la guerre [du Vietnam], mais ce qui
me gênait, c'est que ceux qui la faisaient en
devenaient les victimes. »
Robert De Niro

STILL FROM 'THE DEER HUNTER' (1978)
Michael seems the most well-equipped for Vietnam,
both psychologically and physically, but is he a hero or
a violent misfit? / Sowohl psychisch als auch physisch
scheint Michael am besten von allen für Vietnam
gerüstet – doch ist er wirklich ein Held oder nur ein
gewalttätiger Außenseiter? / Apparemment le mieux
équipé, tant physiquement que psychologiquement,
pour affronter le Vietnam, Michael est-il un héros ou un
dangereux marginal ?

PAGES 56/57
STILL FROM 'THE DEER HUNTER' (1978)
The Vietnam war is a metaphor for the uncontrolled
personal rage of the characters. / Der Vietnamkrieg
dient als Metapher für die unkontrollierte innere Wut
der Charaktere. / La guerre du Vietnam sert de
métaphore à la rage incontrôlée des personnages.

ON THE SET OF 'THE DEER HUNTER' (1978)
With director Michael Cimino on the set. / Mit
Regisseur Michael Cimino bei den Dreharbeiten. / Sur
le tournage avec le réalisateur Michael Cimino.

STILL FROM 'THE DEER HUNTER' (1978)
Michael and Steven (John Savage) try to escape.
The actors did this very dangerous stunt. / Michael
und Steven (John Savage) versuchen zu fliehen. Die
Schauspieler drehten diesen sehr gefährlichen Stunt
selbst. / Les deux comédiens effectuent eux-mêmes
cette cascade périlleuse, dans la scène où Michael et
Steven (John Savage) tentent de s'enfuir.

ON THE SET OF 'RAGING BULL' (1980)
De Niro as boxer Jake La Motta with the real La Motta.
De Niro nurtured the project, spent two years on
research, and was personally trained by La Motta. /
De Niro als Boxer Jake La Motta mit dem echten
La Motta. De Niro hätschelte dieses Projekt, verbrachte
zwei Jahre mit Recherchen und wurde von La Motta
persönlich trainiert. / De Niro aux côtés du boxeur
Jake La Motta, dont il interprète le rôle et qui l'a
personnellement entraîné au cours de ses deux ans
de préparation.

STILL FROM 'RAGING BULL' (1980)
De Niro evokes one of director Martin Scorsese's
cinematic heroes in this shot: John Garfield from 'Body
and Soul' (1947). / De Niro erinnert in dieser Einstellung
an einen von Martin Scorseses Kinohelden: John
Garfield in *Jagd nach Millionen* (1947). / Dans ce plan,
De Niro ressemble à l'un des personnages favoris du
réalisateur Martin Scorsese : John Garfield dans
Sang et Or (1947).

PAGES 62 & 63
STILLS FROM 'RAGING BULL' (1980)
Jake is punished for his sins in this quasi-religious
parable of redemption. / In dieser quasireligiösen
Erlösungsparabel wird Jake für seine Sünden bestraft. /
Dans cette parabole quasi religieuse sur la rédemption,
Jake est puni pour ses péchés.

STILL FROM 'RAGING BULL' (1980)
Violence on the home front mirrors the violence in the
boxing ring. / Die Gewalt an der „Heimatfront" spiegelt
die Gewalt im Boxring. / La violence domestique fait
écho à la violence du ring.

STILL FROM 'RAGING BULL' (1980)
De Niro gained 70 pounds to play the older Jake, and
won an Academy Award. Physical transformation is an
important part of De Niro's acting process. / De Niro
nahm 32 Kilogramm zu, um den älteren Jake zu spielen,
und gewann einen Academy Award. Die körperliche
Wandlung ist für De Niro ein wichtiger Teil des
Schauspielens. / L'acteur, dont le jeu repose en partie
sur la transformation physique, prend 30 kilos en même
temps que son personnage et est récompensé par
un oscar.

PAGES 66/67
STILL FROM 'TRUE CONFESSIONS' (1981)
Catholic guilt and redemption inform many of De Niro's characterizations, including his portrayal of ambitious Father Des Spellacy, here with his detective brother (Robert Duvall). / Katholische Vorstellungen von Schuld und Erlösung stecken in vielen von De Niros Rollen – wie in dieser Darstellung des ehrgeizigen Priesters Des Spellacy, hier mit seinem Bruder (Robert Duvall), einem Kripobeamten. / Les notions catholiques de culpabilité et de rédemption imprègnent beaucoup des personnages de De Niro, notamment l'ambitieux père Des Spellacy, ici avec son frère détective (Robert Duvall).

STILL FROM 'THE KING OF COMEDY' (1983)
Rupert Pupkin (De Niro) is a deluded struggling comedian who kidnaps talk-show host Jerry Langford to get a spot on TV. "Better to be king for a night than schmuck for a lifetime." / Rupert Pupkin (De Niro) ist ein ebenso verblendeter wie erfolgloser Komiker, der den Talkshowmoderator Jerry Langford entführt, um endlich ins Fernsehen zu kommen. „Besser eine Nacht lang König als ein Leben lang Trottel." / Convaincu de son talent, l'humoriste vedette Rupert Pupkin (De Niro) kidnappe l'animateur vedette Jerry Langford pour passer dans son émission. « Mieux vaut être un roi d'un soir qu'un raté toute sa vie. »

STILL FROM 'THE KING OF COMEDY' (1983)
Jerry Langford (Jerry Lewis) in one of Rupert's dreams.
The film, developed by De Niro and presented to
director Martin Scorsese, takes a mordant look at self-
delusion and celebrity worship. / Jerry Langford (Jerry
Lewis) in einem von Ruperts Träumen. Der Film, den
De Niro selbst entwickelte und dann Regisseur Martin
Scorsese vorstellte, nimmt Selbsttäuschung und
Promikult bissig auf die Schippe. / Jerry Langford
(Jerry Lewis) dans l'un des rêves de Rupert. Conçu par
De Niro et réalisé par Martin Scorsese, ce film jette un
regard mordant sur l'aveuglement et le culte de la
célébrité.

STILL FROM 'FALLING IN LOVE' (1984)
Molly Gilmore (Meryl Streep) and Frank Raftis (De Niro)
keep meeting in New York and start to fall in love,
but cannot bring themselves to leave their respective
partners. / Molly Gilmore (Meryl Streep) und Frank
Raftis (De Niro) laufen sich in New York immer wieder
über den Weg und beginnen, sich ineinander zu
verlieben, können sich aber nicht überwinden, ihre
jeweiligen Partner zu verlassen. / Molly Gilmore (Meryl
Streep) et Frank Raftis (De Niro), qui ne cessent de se
croiser dans New York, finissent par tomber amoureux
sans pouvoir se résoudre à quitter leurs époux
respectifs.

STILL FROM 'FALLING IN LOVE' (1984)
Meryl Streep has known De Niro for some time: "Bob
has always been very loyal to me, during a really hard
time in my life, and I feel I can count on him. But deeply,
I don't know him. He is a very kind of unto-himself
person, too." / Meryl Streep kannte De Niro schon eine
Weile: „Bob hielt sehr treu zu mir während einer sehr
schwierigen Zeit in meinem Leben, und ich habe das
Gefühl, ich kann mich auf ihn verlassen. Aber im tiefsten
Inneren kenne ich ihn nicht. Er ist auch ein Mensch, der
sehr stark in sich gekehrt ist." / « Bob a toujours été très
loyal envers moi à une époque très dure de ma vie et je
sens que je peux compter sur lui », confie Meryl Streep,
qui le connaît depuis assez longtemps. « Mais au fond,
je ne sais rien de lui. C'est quelqu'un de très secret. »

STILL FROM 'ONCE UPON A TIME IN AMERICA' (1984)
Attracted to Italian director Sergio Leone's visual sense, De Niro joined this film about Jewish gangsters in America. / Weil er vom visuellen Stil des italienischen Regisseurs Sergio Leone fasziniert war, machte De Niro bei diesem Film über jüdische Gangster in Amerika mit. / Attiré par l'esthétique du cinéaste italien Sergio Leone, De Niro accepte ce rôle de gangster juif.

"The talent is in the choices."
Robert De Niro

„Talent besteht darin, richtig auszuwählen."
Robert De Niro

« Le talent est dans les choix qu'on fait. »
Robert De Niro

STILL FROM 'ONCE UPON A TIME IN AMERICA' (1984)
Leone brought his trademark operatic style to the film.
David "Noodles" Aaronson (De Niro) relaxes in luxury
with his lifelong love, Deborah (Elizabeth McGovern). /
Leone brachte seinen charakteristischen opernhaften
Stil in den Film ein. David „Noodles" Aaronson (De Niro)
entspannt sich stilgerecht mit der Liebe seines Lebens,
Deborah (Elizabeth McGovern). / Avec la démesure
légendaire de Sergio Leone, David Aaronson alias
«Noodles» (De Niro) se détend avec son amour de
toujours, Deborah (Elizabeth McGovern).

STILL FROM 'ONCE UPON A TIME IN AMERICA' (1984)
Noodles is released from prison in this brutal meditation on friendship and betrayal. / „Noodles" wird in dieser brutalen Abhandlung über Freundschaft und Verrat aus dem Gefängnis entlassen. / Noodles à sa sortie de prison, dans une brutale histoire d'amitié et de trahison.

STILL FROM 'ONCE UPON A TIME IN AMERICA' (1984)
At the end of the film, Noodles confronts his erstwhile friend Max Bercovicz (James Woods). / Am Ende des Films stellt „Noodles" seinen einstigen Freund Max Bercovicz (James Woods) zur Rede. / À la fin du film, Noodles règle ses comptes avec son ancien ami Max Bercovicz (James Woods).

STILL FROM 'BRAZIL' (1985)
Although it was a cameo appearance, De Niro did a lot
of research, made many costume and prop changes, and
took two weeks to film. / Obwohl es sich nur um eine
Cameo-Rolle handelte, recherchierte De Niro ausgiebig,
veränderte Kostüme und Requisiten und nahm sich
zwei Wochen Zeit für die Dreharbeiten. / Bien qu'il ne
fasse qu'une brève apparition, De Niro effectue
d'innombrables recherches, fait remanier maintes fois
les costumes et les accessoires et consacre quinze jours
au tournage.

*"There is a certain combination of anarchy and
discipline in the way I work."*
Robert De Niro

*„In meiner Arbeitsweise gibt es eine gewisse
Kombination aus Anarchie und Disziplin."*
Robert De Niro

*« Il y a un mélange d'anarchie et de discipline dans
ma façon de travailler. »*
Robert De Niro

STILL FROM 'THE MISSION' (1986)
Rodrigo Mendoza (De Niro) returns with his latest batch
of slaves. To him they are just things to be captured and
sold, like wild animals. / Rodrigo Mendoza (De Niro)
kehrt mit seiner Beute von seinem jüngsten Sklaven-
fang zurück. Für ihn sind sie nichts weiter als Objekte,
die man einfängt und verkauft, wie wilde Tiere. /
Rodrigo Mendoza (De Niro) ramène un nouveau lot
d'esclaves. Pour lui, ce ne sont rien de plus que des
objets qu'il s'agit de capturer et de revendre, tels des
animaux sauvages.

STILL FROM 'THE MISSION' (1986)
Slave trader Rodrigo Mendoza kills his brother in a fit
of rage over Carlotta (Cherie Lunghi). / Der Sklaven-
händler Rodrigo Mendoza tötet seinen Bruder in einem
Wutanfall, weil Carlotta (Cherie Lunghi) diesen mehr
begehrt als ihn. / Par amour pour Carlotta (Cherie
Lunghi), le marchand d'esclaves Rodrigo Mendoza tue
son frère dans un terrible accès de jalousie.

STILL FROM 'THE MISSION' (1986)
De Niro, in a tale of guilt and redemption, walks
barefoot across jagged rocks. / De Niro läuft in dieser
Geschichte über Schuld und Erlösung barfuß über
spitze Steine. / Dans cette fable sur la culpabilité et la
rédemption, De Niro marche pieds nus sur des rochers
escarpés.

STILL FROM 'THE MISSION' (1986)
Looking for forgiveness, Mendoza creates his own
dangerous "way of the cross"—carrying his armor to the
top of a mountain—aided by Father Gabriel (Jeremy
Irons). / Auf der Suche nach Vergebung erschafft
Mendoza seinen eigenen „Kreuzweg", indem er,
unterstützt von Pater Gabriel (Jeremy Irons), seine
Rüstung auf einen Berg schleppt. / En quête de
rédemption, Mendoza gravit son propre « chemin de
croix » en transportant son armure au sommet de la
montagne avec l'aide du frère Gabriel (Jeremy Irons).

*"He's a very shy man and takes a lot of getting to
know, so I suppose our off-screen relationship
mirrored our on-screen one."*
Jeremy Irons, actor

*„Er ist ein sehr schüchterner Mensch, und es dauert
lange, bis man ihn richtig kennenlernt. Ich denke
daher, dass unser Verhältnis abseits der Kameras
ein Spiegelbild dessen war, was wir vor der Kamera
spielten."*
Jeremy Irons, Schauspieler

STILL FROM 'THE MISSION' (1986)
The Indians sever the armor and Mendoza is redeemed
at last. / Die Indios befreien ihn von seiner Last, und
Mendoza findet schließlich seine Erlösung. / Les Indiens
ayant sectionné l'armure, Mendoza se rachète enfin.

*« C'est un homme très timide qu'il faut apprendre
à connaître ; on peut donc dire que notre relation
hors écran reflétait notre relation à l'écran. »*
Jeremy Irons, acteur

STILL FROM 'THE UNTOUCHABLES' (1987)
De Palma and De Niro, together again, as De Niro lets
his demonic side loose as the ruthless Al Capone. /
De Palma und De Niro sind wieder vereint, als De Niro
in der Rolle des skrupellosen Al Capone seiner
dämonischen Seite freien Lauf lassen kann. / De Palma
et De Niro, de nouveau réunis, laissent libre cours au
côté démoniaque de l'acteur dans le rôle de
l'impitoyable Al Capone.

PORTRAIT FOR 'ANGEL HEART' (1987)
De Niro incarnates the Devil in Alan Parker's erotic,
mystical allegory. / In Alan Parkers erotisch-mystischer
Allegorie spielt De Niro den Teufel. / De Niro incarne le
Diable dans cette allégorie mystico-érotique signée
Alan Parker.

STILL FROM 'MIDNIGHT RUN' (1988)
De Niro adeptly combines comedy and drama in his
role as the bitter bounty hunter Jack Walsh, here with
his prey—Jonathan Mardukas (Charles Grodin). /
De Niro verknüpft in seiner Rolle als verbitterter
Kopfgeldjäger Jack Walsh – hier mit seiner Beute,
Jonathan Mardukas (Charles Grodin) – geschickt
Komödie und Drama. / De Niro allie comédie et drame
dans le rôle du chasseur de primes Jack Walsh, ici en
compagnie de sa proie, Jonathan Mardukas
(Charles Grodin).

STILL FROM 'JACKNIFE' (1989)
Troubled Vietnam veteran Joseph "Jacknife" Megessey,
who is renowned for punching his hand through
windows, tries to help out fellow vet David Flannigan
(Ed Harris). / Der mit Problemen beladene Vietnam-
Veteran Joseph „Jacknife" Megessey, der dafür bekannt
ist, mit seiner Faust Fensterscheiben zu durchschlagen,
versucht seinem alten Kameraden David Flannigan
(Ed Harris) zu helfen. / Le vétéran du Vietnam Joseph
Megessey alias « Jacknife », qui a la fâcheuse manie de
briser des vitres à main nue, tente d'aider son frère
d'armes David Flannigan (Ed Harris).

STILL FROM 'WE'RE NO ANGELS' (1989)
De Niro mugs shamelessly for the benefit of Molly
(Demi Moore) in Neil Jordan's remake of the Humphrey
Bogart comedy 'We're No Angels' (1955). / De Niro
schämt sich nicht, vor Molly (Demi Moore) Grimassen
zu ziehen in Neil Jordans Remake der Humphrey-
Bogart-Komödie *Wir sind keine Engel* (1955) von Michael
Curtiz. / De Niro grimace impudemment pour les beaux
yeux de Molly (Demi Moore) dans le remake signé Neil
Jordan de la comédie de Michael Curtiz *La Cuisine des
anges* (1955) avec Humphrey Bogart.

STILL FROM 'AWAKENINGS' (1990)
In another transformative role, De Niro plays Leonard
Lowe, a victim of a sleeping disease who is suddenly
awakened by a radical new treatment. The film was
based on Dr. Oliver Sacks's psychiatric study. / In einer
weiteren Rolle, die ihn stark veränderte, spielt De Niro
Leonard Lowe, der an der Schlafkrankheit leidet und
durch eine radikal neue Behandlungsmethode plötzlich
wieder zum Leben erwacht. Der Film basiert auf der
psychiatrischen Studie von Oliver Sacks. / Nouvelle
métamorphose pour le rôle de Leonard Lowe, patient
atteint d'une maladie léthargique et soudain réveillé par
un nouveau traitement. Le film s'inspire d'une étude
psychiatrique du Dr Oliver Sacks.

"There's often this tendency with actors when they're asked to play a villainous part to send little signals to the audience that say, 'I'm not really like this.' De Niro doesn't do that."
Sean Connery, actor

„Schauspieler, die einen Bösewicht spielen sollen, neigen oft dazu, dem Publikum kleine Signale zu senden, die sagen: ‚In Wirklichkeit bin ich nicht so.' De Niro tut das nicht."
Sean Connery, Schauspieler

« Lorsqu'ils jouent des rôles de méchants, les acteurs ont souvent tendance à envoyer de petits signaux au public pour dire : "Je ne suis pas réellement comme ça." Ce n'est pas le cas de De Niro. »
Sean Connery, acteur

PORTRAIT FOR 'GOODFELLAS' (1990)
De Niro, as Jimmy Conway, takes a supporting role in Scorsese's landmark study of Mafia wiseguys: Henry Hill (Ray Liotta), Paul Cicero (Paul Sorvino), and Tommy DeVito (Joe Pesci). / De Niro spielt als Jimmy Conway eine Nebenrolle in Scorseses bahnbrechender Mafiastudie: Henry Hill (Ray Liotta), Paul Cicero (Paul Sorvino) und Tommy DeVito (Joe Pesci). / De Niro dans le rôle secondaire de Jimmy Conway aux côtés d'autres affranchis, Henry Hill (Ray Liotta), Paul Cicero (Paul Sorvino) et Tommy DeVito (Joe Pesci) dans le célèbre film de Scorsese consacré à la mafia.

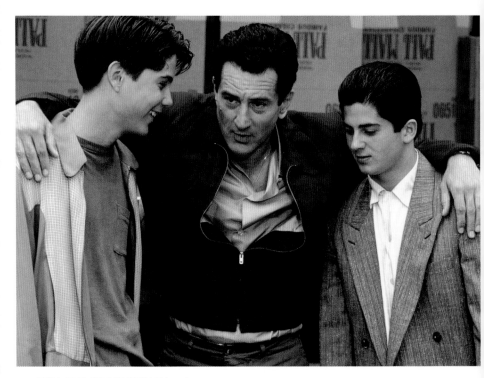

STILL FROM 'GOODFELLAS' (1990)
Jimmy Conway takes the young Henry and Tommy
under his wing and shows them the tricks of the trade. /
Jimmy Conway nimmt Henry und Tommy in jungen
Jahren unter seine Fittiche und bringt ihnen die Tricks
seines Metiers bei. / Jimmy Conway prend les jeunes
Henry et Tommy sous son aile pour leur apprendre les
ficelles du métier.

STILL FROM 'GOODFELLAS' (1990)
The film's graphic violence brought both criticism and
praise. / Die drastische Gewalt brachte dem Film
sowohl Lob als auch Kritik ein. / La violence crue du film
lui vaut autant de critiques que d'éloges.

PAGES 92/93
ON THE SET OF 'GOODFELLAS' (1990)
According to many observers, De Niro and Scorsese
became like one person on the set, communicating
intimately, sometimes to the exclusion of others. / Für
viele Beobachter wurden De Niro und Scorsese bei den
Dreharbeiten eins: Sie kommunizierten so intim
miteinander, dass andere mitunter ausgeschlossen
blieben. / Selon de nombreux témoins, De Niro et
Scorsese ne font plus qu'un sur le plateau et
communiquent si intimement que les autres finissent
par se sentir exclus.

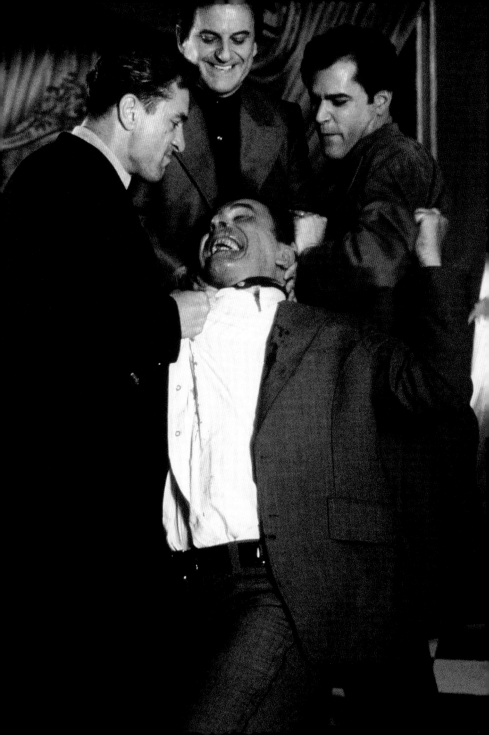

"I think Hollywood has a class system. The actors are like the inmates, but the truth is they're running the asylum."
Robert De Niro

„Ich denke, in Hollywood herrscht ein Klassensystem. Die Schauspieler sind wie die Insassen, aber in Wirklichkeit haben sie in der Irrenanstalt das Sagen."
Robert De Niro

« Hollywood possède un système de classes. Les acteurs semblent être les pensionnaires, mais en réalité, ce sont eux qui dirigent l'asile. »
Robert De Niro

STILL FROM 'STANLEY & IRIS' (1990)
De Niro returns to romance, this time with a working-class ambience. The illiterate Stanley (De Niro) romances his feisty teacher Iris (Jane Fonda). /
De Niro kehrt wieder zum Liebesfilm zurück – diesmal im Arbeitermilieu angesiedelt: Analphabet Stanley (De Niro) schwärmt für seine resolute Lehrerin Iris (Jane Fonda). / Retour à la comédie sentimentale, cette fois dans un milieu populaire, avec l'histoire de Stanley (De Niro), un illettré auquel la vaillante Iris (Jane Fonda) décide d'apprendre à lire.

STILL FROM 'GUILTY BY SUSPICION' (1991)
Film director David Merrill (De Niro) is blacklisted when
he refuses to cooperate with the Communist witch hunt
in 1950s America. / Filmregisseur David Merrill (De Niro)
wird auf die Schwarze Liste gesetzt, als er sich weigert,
an der Hexenjagd auf Kommunisten im Amerika der
1950er-Jahre teilzunehmen. / Le cinéaste David Merrill
(De Niro) est placé sur liste noire pour avoir refusé de
coopérer à la chasse aux sorcières dans l'Amérique
maccarthyste.

STILL FROM 'BACKDRAFT' (1991)
De Niro occasionally took supporting roles to support
his growing investments in the revitalization of the
Tribeca neighborhood in New York City. Here arson
investigator Donald Rimgale (De Niro) talks with Brian
McCaffrey (William Baldwin). / De Niro übernahm
gelegentlich Nebenrollen, um seine wachsenden
Investitionen in den New Yorker Stadtteil Tribeca zu
finanzieren. Donald Rimgale (De Niro), der für die
Untersuchung von Brandstiftungen zuständig ist, spricht
hier mit Brian McCaffrey (William Baldwin). / Acceptant
des rôles secondaires pour financer ses efforts de
revitalisation du quartier new-yorkais de Tribeca,
De Niro joue ici un enquêteur de la brigade des
incendies criminels, Donald Rimgale, aux côtés de Brian
McCaffrey (William Baldwin).

PAGES 98 & 99
STILLS FROM 'CAPE FEAR' (1991)
Convicted rapist Max Cady (De Niro) abuses Lori
Davis (Illeana Douglas). De Niro transformed himself
into an Old Testament angel of death for Martin
Scorsese's extravagant homage to the original noir
classic 'Cape Fear' (1962). / Der verurteilte Triebtäter
Max Cady (De Niro) misshandelt Lori Davis (Illeana
Douglas). De Niro verwandelte sich für Martin
Scorseses extravagante Hommage an den *Film-noir*-
Klassiker *Ein Köder für die Bestie* (1962) in einen
alttestamentarischen Todesengel. / Dans le rôle du
violeur Max Cady, qui agresse ici Lori Davis (Illeana
Douglas), De Niro se transforme en ange exterminateur
sorti de l'Ancien Testament pour l'extravagant
hommage de Martin Scorsese au célèbre film noir
Les Nerfs à vif (1962).

"I think Bobby and Marty [Scorsese] are like brothers. There's something about Bobby being Marty's alter ego. Marty allows Bobby to do the violence; he allows him to be the hit man, so to speak."
Steven Spielberg, director

„Ich denke, Bobby und Marty [Scorsese] sind wie Brüder. Man könnte Bobby auch als Martys Alter Ego betrachten. Marty überlässt Bobby die Gewaltszenen – er gestattet ihm sozusagen, der Auftragskiller zu sein."
Steven Spielberg, Regisseur

« Bobby et Marty [Scorsese] sont comme deux frères. On dirait que Bobby est l'alter ego de Marty. Marty laisse Bobby se charger de la violence ; c'est en quelque sorte son homme de main. »
Steven Spielberg, réalisateur

STILL FROM 'CAPE FEAR' (1991)
Max Cady assures self-righteous and hypocritical lawyer Sam Bowden (Nick Nolte) that he and his family will know the meaning of loss. Ironically, by being tested to their breaking point, the dysfunctional Bowdens actually form a stronger family unit at the end. / Max Cady versichert dem selbstgerechten und heuchlerischen Rechtsanwalt Sam Bowden (Nick Nolte), dass auch er und seine Familie erfahren werden, was „Verlust" bedeutet. Ironischerweise schweißt diese harte Prüfung, die sie an die Grenzen ihrer Belastbarkeit bringt, die zerrüttete Familie am Ende des Films viel enger zusammen. / Face à Max Cady, qui a juré de se venger sur sa famille, son avocat Sam Bowden (Nick Nolte), hypocrite et bien-pensant, vit un calvaire qui finira curieusement par resserrer les liens du ménage.

STILL FROM 'NIGHT AND THE CITY' (1992)
Ambulance-chasing lawyer Harry Fabian (De Niro) is menaced by "Boom Boom" Grossman (Alan King) in a weak remake of a film-noir classic. / Winkeladvokat Harry Fabian (De Niro) wird von „Boom Boom" Grossman (Alan King) bedroht in einem schwachen Remake des *Film-noir*-Klassikers *Die Ratte von Soho* (1950). / Dans ce médiocre remake d'un classique du film noir, *Les Forbans de la nuit* (1950), l'avocat véreux Harry Fabian (De Niro) est menacé par « Boom Boom » Grossman (Alan King).

STILL FROM 'MISTRESS' (1992)
Entrepreneur Evan M. Wright (De Niro) is asked to finance a film in the first production of De Niro's Tribeca Productions. / In diesem ersten Film von De Niros eigener Produktionsfirma Tribeca wird der Unternehmer Evan M. Wright (De Niro) gebeten, einen Film zu finanzieren. / Dans le premier film produit par sa propre maison, Tribeca Productions, De Niro incarne l'homme d'affaires Evan M. Wright, sollicité pour financer un film.

STILL FROM 'MAD DOG AND GLORY' (1993)
Mild-mannered police photographer Wayne "Mad Dog"
Dobie saves the life of mobster Frank Milo (Bill Murray),
who wishes to show his appreciation. / Der sanftmütige
Fotograf Wayne „Mad Dog" Dobie rettet das Leben des
Mafioso Frank Milo (Bill Murray), der sich dankbar
zeigen möchte. / Le gangster Frank Milo (Bill Murray)
tient à montrer sa gratitude au photographe de la police
Wayne Dobie, alias « Mad Dog », qui lui a sauvé la vie.

*"It's important not to indicate. People don't try
to show their feelings, they try to hide them."*
Robert De Niro

*„Es ist wichtig, keine Fingerzeige zu geben.
Die Menschen versuchen nicht, ihre Gefühle
zu zeigen. Sie versuchen, sie zu verbergen."*
Robert De Niro

*« Il ne faut pas être démonstratif. Les gens
n'essaient pas de montrer leurs sentiments,
ils tentent au contraire de les cacher. »*
Robert De Niro

STILL FROM 'MAD DOG AND GLORY' (1993)
Milo lends his employee Glory (Uma Thurman) to Dobie
for a week, forcing the shy police photographer to come
out of his shell. / Milo „verleiht" seine Angestellte Glory
(Uma Thurman) eine Woche lang an Dobie und zwingt
den schüchternen Polizeifotografen so, aus sich
herauszukommen. / Milo prête son employée Glory
(Uma Thurman) à Dobie pour une semaine, forçant le
timide photographe de police à sortir de sa coquille.

PAGES 106/107
STILL FROM 'THIS BOY'S LIFE' (1993)
Overbearing Dwight Hansen (De Niro) is short-
tempered and accustomed to being obeyed, as his
stepson Toby (Leonardo DiCaprio) finds out. / Der
herrische Dwight Hansen (De Niro) ist leicht reizbar
und gewohnt, dass man ihm gehorcht, wie sein
Stiefsohn Toby (Leonardo DiCaprio) erfahren muss. /
Dwight Hansen (De Niro) est un homme autoritaire et
colérique habitué à être obéi, comme le découvre son
beau-fils Toby (Leonardo DiCaprio).

STILL FROM 'THIS BOY'S LIFE' (1993)
Dwight teaches Toby how to beat up people. / Dwight
lehrt Toby, wie man Menschen zusammenschlägt. /
Dwight apprend à Toby à se battre.

"He was so honest and so emotionally open that
the other actors had to run to keep up with him."
Michael Caton-Jones, director

„Er war so ehrlich und emotional so offen, dass sich
die anderen Schauspieler anstrengen mussten, um
mit ihm Schritt zu halten."
Michael Caton-Jones, Regisseur

« Il était tellement honnête et émotionnellement
ouvert que les autres acteurs étaient contraints de
courir pour ne pas se laisser distancer. »
Michael Caton-Jones, réalisateur

STILL FROM 'THIS BOY'S LIFE' (1993)
Garage mechanic Dwight can also be charming, which makes it easy for Toby's mother to turn a blind eye to his abusive nature. / Der Kfz-Mechaniker Dwight hat auch eine charmante Seite, die es Tobys Mutter leichtmacht, über sein aufbrausendes Wesen hinwegzusehen. / Dwight sait également être charmant, ce qui permet à la mère de Toby de fermer les yeux sur le caractère violent de son mécanicien de mari.

STILL FROM 'A BRONX TALE' (1993)
In his first film as director, De Niro plays Bronx bus
driver Lorenzo Anello who tries to bring up his son
Calogero (Lillo Brancato) with the proper morals. /
In seinem ersten Film als Regisseur spielt De Niro den
Busfahrer Lorenzo Anello aus der Bronx, der versucht,
seinen Sohn Calogero (Lillo Brancato) mit der richtigen
moralischen Einstellung zu erziehen. / Dans son
premier film en tant que réalisateur, De Niro incarne
Lorenzo Anello, chauffeur de bus du Bronx qui tente
d'inculquer à son fils Calogero (Lillo Brancato) le
respect des valeurs morales.

STILL FROM 'A BRONX TALE' (1993)
Gangster Sonny LoSpecchio, played by writer Chazz
Palminteri, is idolized by the young Calogero (Francis
Capra). / Gangster Sonny LoSpecchio, dargestellt von
Autor Chazz Palminteri, wird von dem jungen Calogero
(Francis Capra) vergöttert. / Le mafioso Sonny
LoSpecchio, interprété par Chazz Palminteri - qui a
également signé le scénario du film - est idolâtré par
le jeune Calogero (Francis Capra).

STILL FROM 'A BRONX TALE' (1993)
When Calogero refuses to grass Sonny to the police,
Sonny takes Calogero under his wing and teaches him
about life on the street. / Als Calogero sich weigert,
Sonny an die Polizei zu verpfeifen, nimmt der Gangster
ihn unter seine Fittiche und erzählt ihm vom Leben auf
der Straße. / Calogero ayant refusé de dénoncer Sonny
à la police, le gangster le considère comme son fils
adoptif et lui apprend les règles du milieu.

STILL FROM 'A BRONX TALE' (1993)
The confrontation between the two fathers.
Relationships between fathers and sons begin to
become a common theme in De Niro's choice of
projects, reflecting his own burgeoning parenthood. /
Die Konfrontation zwischen den beiden Vätern. Vater-
Sohn-Beziehungen werden zu einem übergreifenden
Thema in den Filmen, die sich De Niro aussucht –
ein Spiegel seiner eigenen Vaterschaft. / Confrontation entre les deux pères. Comme en écho à sa
propre paternité, les relations entre pères et fils
deviennent un thème récurrent dans les films choisis
par De Niro.

*"The thing that really makes him great is that he
can concentrate harder than anybody I have ever
seen."*
Chazz Palminteri, scriptwriter-actor

*„Was ihn wirklich groß macht, ist, dass er sich
stärker konzentrieren kann als jeder andere, den
ich gesehen habe."*
Chazz Palminteri, Drehbuchautor und Schauspieler

*« Ce qui le rend vraiment extraordinaire, c'est qu'il
possède une capacité de concentration hors du
commun. »*
Chazz Palminteri, scénariste et acteur

STILL FROM 'FRANKENSTEIN' (1994)
The Creature confronts his irresponsible creator, Victor
Frankenstein (Kenneth Branagh), in this moral allegory. /
Das Geschöpf stellt seinen verantwortungslosen
Schöpfer Victor Frankenstein (Kenneth Branagh) in
dieser Moralallegorie zur Rede. / Une allégorie morale
où la Créature s'en prend à son irresponsable créateur,
Victor Frankenstein (Kenneth Branagh).

STILL FROM 'FRANKENSTEIN' (1994)
De Niro brings a unique psychological take to his
portrayal of Mary Shelley's Creature. / De Niro verleiht
seiner Darstellung von Mary Shelleys Kreatur eine
einzigartige psychologische Note. / De Niro confère
une dimension psychologique inédite à la Créature de
Mary Shelley.

STILL FROM 'CASINO' (1995)
Martin Scorsese and Robert De Niro investigate the
Las Vegas Mob. The film begins with Sam "Ace"
Rothstein (De Niro) being car-bombed. / Martin
Scorsese und Robert De Niro nehmen sich die Mafia
von Las Vegas vor. Der Film beginnt mit einem
Autobombenanschlag auf Sam „Ace" Rothstein
(De Niro). / Attaque à la voiture piégée contre Sam
Rothstein alias « Ace » (De Niro) au début du film de
Martin Scorsese consacré à la mafia de Las Vegas.

STILL FROM 'CASINO' (1995)
Ace is a precise and meticulous man who knows all the
tricks. His job is to ensure that the Mob-controlled
Tangiers casino will make the maximum profit for his
bosses. / „Ace" ist ein akribischer und sorgfältiger
Mensch, der sämtliche Tricks kennt. Seine Aufgabe ist
es sicherzustellen, dass das von der Mafia kontrollierte
Tangiers-Kasino den größtmöglichen Gewinn für seine
Bosse abwirft. / Homme précis et méticuleux
connaissant toutes les ficelles, Ace veille à la rentabilité
de l'hôtel-casino Tangiers, contrôlé par la mafia.

ON THE SET OF 'CASINO' (1995)
Robert De Niro and Don Rickles, playing Ace's casino
manager, walk through a scene. / Robert De Niro und
Don Rickles, der den Geschäftsführer des Kasinos
spielt, bei den Dreharbeiten zu einer Szene. /
Répétition d'une scène entre Robert De Niro et Don
Rickles, qui incarne le gérant du casino.

*"People treat me with a bit too much reverence.
Look at Dustin Hoffman. I always envy the way he
can speak and be smart and funny and so on. I just
can't do that."*
Robert De Niro

*„Die Leute behandeln mich mit etwas zu viel
Ehrfurcht. Schauen Sie sich Dustin Hoffman an! Ich
beneide immer die Art, wie er reden kann und klug
und witzig ist. Ich kann das einfach nicht."*
Robert De Niro

*« On me traite toujours avec un peu trop de
respect. Regardez Dustin Hoffman. J'ai toujours
envié son aisance verbale, sa capacité à être
intelligent et drôle. Moi, j'en suis incapable. »*
Robert De Niro

ON THE SET OF 'CASINO' (1995)
Martin Scorsese, Joe Pesci, and Robert De Niro working in the Vegas desert. / Martin Scorsese, Joe Pesci und Robert De Niro bei der Arbeit in der Wüste um Las Vegas. / Martin Scorsese, Joe Pesci et Robert De Niro dans le désert non loin de Las Vegas.

PAGES 122/123
STILL FROM 'HEAT' (1995)
The first on-screen pairing of the two most prestigious actors of their generation, Pacino and De Niro, playing driven characters on opposite sides of the law. / Der erste gemeinsame Leinwandauftritt der zwei größten Schauspieler ihrer Generation, Pacino und De Niro, die getriebene Charaktere auf unterschiedlichen Seiten des Gesetzes spielen. / Le premier face-à-face des deux plus grands acteurs de leur génération, Pacino et De Niro, dans des personnages habités de flic et de truand.

STILL FROM 'CASINO' (1995)
Ace marries hustler and femme fatale Ginger McKenna (Sharon Stone), the one element in his life Rothstein cannot effectively control. / „Ace" heiratet die Prostituierte und Femme fatale Ginger McKenna (Sharon Stone), das Einzige in seinem Leben, das Rothstein nicht wirklich im Griff hat. / Ace épouse la femme fatale Ginger McKenna (Sharon Stone), le seul élément de sa vie qu'il ne peut contrôler.

STILL FROM 'HEAT' (1995)
Neil McCauley (De Niro) leads a bank robbery that
goes horribly, and violently, wrong. Chris Shiherlis
(Val Kilmer) provides covering fire. / Neil McCauley
(De Niro) führt einen Bankraub an, der fürchterlich und
blutig schiefläuft. Chris Shiherlis (Val Kilmer) gibt ihm
Deckung. / Neil McCauley (De Niro), couvert par son
complice Chris Shiherlis (Val Kilmer), mène une attaque
de banque qui tourne mal.

STILL FROM 'HEAT' (1995)
The loneliness of the criminal who wants out, painted in
neon blue, an image typical of director Michael Mann. /
Die Einsamkeit des Kriminellen, der aussteigen möchte,
gemalt in Neonblau – ein für Regisseur Michael Mann
typisches Bild. / Le criminel enfermé dans sa solitude,
dans une lumière bleutée caractéristique du réalisateur
Michael Mann.

STILL FROM 'SLEEPERS' (1996)
Father Bobby (De Niro) lies under oath in this tale of
institutional corruption and child abuse. / Pater Bobby
(De Niro) lügt unter Eid in dieser Geschichte über
institutionelle Korruption und Kindesmisshandlung. /
Le père Bobby (De Niro) fait un faux témoignage dans
ce film sur la corruption institutionnelle et les abus
sexuels dans les prisons pour mineurs.

STILL FROM 'MARVIN'S ROOM' (1996)
De Niro convinced Meryl Streep and Diane Keaton
(pictured) to participate in this film, which he co-
produced and played a small part in. / De Niro
überzeugte Meryl Streep und Diane Keaton (im Bild)
zur Mitwirkung in diesem Film, den er koproduzierte
und in dem er eine kleine Rolle spielte. / De Niro
convainc Meryl Streep et Diane Keaton (en photo) de
participer à ce film, qu'il coproduit et dans lequel il joue
un petit rôle.

"He appears to have a tremendous potential for
violence. He is one of the more frightening people
I have met in my life ... "
Kenneth Branagh, director-actor

„Er scheint ein ungeheures Gewaltpotenzial zu
besitzen. Er gehört zu den beängstigenderen
Menschen, die ich in meinem Leben kennengelernt
habe ...“
Kenneth Branagh, Regisseur und Schauspieler

« Il semble avoir un extraordinaire potentiel de
violence. C'est l'une des personnes les plus
terrifiantes que j'aie rencontrées dans ma vie... »
Kenneth Branagh, acteur et réalisateur

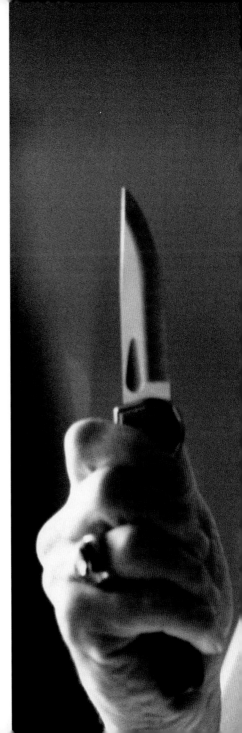

STILL FROM 'THE FAN' (1996)
Gil Renard (De Niro) is a failing hunting-knife salesman,
and an obsessed baseball fan. / Gil Renard (De Niro) ist
als Verkäufer von Jagdmessern eine Niete – und er ist
ein besessener Baseballfan. / Gil Renard (De Niro) est
un piètre représentant en couteaux de chasse obsédé
par le base-ball.

STILL FROM 'THE FAN' (1996)
When Gil is fired from his job, he expends all his
intense energy to ensure that all-star outfielder Bobby
Rayburn has all the help he needs to have a successful
season with the San Francisco Giants. / Als Gil gefeuert
wird, verwendet er seine geballte Energie darauf
sicherzustellen, dass Baseballstar Bobby Rayburn
jede Unterstützung zuteilwird, die er benötigt, um die
San Francisco Giants in dieser Saison zum Erfolg zu
führen. / Renvoyé de son travail, Gil consacre toute
son énergie à son joueur favori, Bobby Rayburn,
afin de lui garantir une saison réussie au sein des
San Francisco Giants.

STILL FROM 'THE FAN' (1996)
The final violent confrontation between Bobby Rayburn (Wesley Snipes) and Gil Renard. / Die abschließende gewalttätige Konfrontation zwischen Bobby Rayburn (Wesley Snipes) und Gil Renard. / La confrontation finale entre Bobby Rayburn (Wesley Snipes) et Gil Renard.

STILL FROM 'COP LAND' (1997)
Internal-affairs investigator Lt. Moe Tilden (De Niro)
tries to help incorruptible small-time sheriff Freddy
Heflin (Sylvester Stallone) track down some crooked
cops. / Lieutenant Moe Tilden (De Niro) ist für
polizeiinterne Untersuchungen zuständig und versucht,
dem unbestechlichen Provinzsheriff Freddy Heflin
(Sylvester Stallone) dabei zu helfen, eine Gruppe
korrupter Polizisten dingfest zu machen. / Moe Tilden
(De Niro), enquêteur de la police des polices, tente
d'aider un incorruptible shérif, Freddy Heflin (Sylvester
Stallone), à poursuivre des flics ripoux.

*"I think playing opposite De Niro is a challenge for
any actor because he is a master of underplaying."*
Cybill Shepherd, actress

*„Ich glaube, eine Hauptrolle neben De Niro
zu haben ist für jeden Schauspieler eine
Herausforderung, weil er ein Meister des
Herunterspielens ist."*
Cybill Shepherd, Schauspielerin

*« Jouer avec De Niro, c'est un challenge pour
n'importe quel acteur, car il est passé maître dans
l'art de sous-jouer. »*
Cybill Shepherd, actrice

STILL FROM 'WAG THE DOG' (1997)
Spin doctor Conrad Brean (De Niro), his associate
Winifred Ames (Anne Heche), and egocentric
Hollywood producer Stanley Motss (Dustin Hoffman)
try to fabricate a war to cover up a sex scandal in this
dead-on political satire directed by Barry Levinson. /
Politpropagandist Conrad Brean (De Niro), seine
Mitarbeiterin Winifred Ames (Anne Heche) und der
egozentrische Hollywood-Produzent Stanley Motss
(Dustin Hoffman) versuchen in dieser treffsicheren
Politsatire von Barry Levinson, einen Krieg vom Zaun zu
brechen, um einen Sexskandal zu vertuschen. / Dans
cette satire politique réalisée par Barry Levinson, le
conseiller en communication Conrad Brean (De Niro),
son associée Winifred Ames (Anne Heche) et le
producteur hollywoodien Stanley Motss (Dustin
Hoffman) tentent de créer une guerre fictive pour
couvrir un scandale sexuel.

STILL FROM 'JACKIE BROWN' (1997)
Postmodern director Quentin Tarantino casts De Niro
as the criminal loser Louis Gara, infatuated with the
duplicitous "beach bunny" Melanie (Bridget Fonda). /
Der postmoderne Regisseur Quentin Tarantino besetzte
mit De Niro die Rolle des kriminellen Verlierers Louis
Gara, der von dem doppelzüngigen „Strandhäschen"
Melanie (Bridget Fonda) angetan ist. / Le cinéaste
postmoderne Quentin Tarantino confie à De Niro le rôle
du criminel désabusé Louis Gara, entiché de la perfide
« pin-up » Melanie (Bridget Fonda).

*"De Niro was it. He was who everyone in my acting
class wanted to be. He was the ideal ... "*
Quentin Tarantino, director

*„De Niro war's. Jeder in meiner Schauspielklasse
wollte so sein wie er. Er war das Ideal ..."*
Quentin Tarantino, Regisseur

*« De Niro, c'était le top. C'est à lui que voulaient
ressembler tous les élèves de mon cours d'art
dramatique. C'était notre idéal... »*
Quentin Tarantino, réalisateur

STILL FROM 'GREAT EXPECTATIONS' (1998)
De Niro gives another extravagant performance as the
prisoner Lustig in a modernization of Charles Dickens's
novel. / De Niro lieferte eine weitere extravagante
Leistung als Gefangener Lustig in einer modernen
Adaption des Romans von Charles Dickens. / Nouveau
numéro d'acteur extravagant pour De Niro dans le rôle
du prisonnier Lustig, dans une adaptation moderne du
roman de Charles Dickens.

STILL FROM 'RONIN' (1998)
Sam (De Niro) is one of a group of mercenaries, including Vincent (Jean Reno), who navigate a maze of violent action scenes in pursuit of a suitcase. / Sam (De Niro) ist Mitglied einer Söldnertruppe, der auch Vincent (Jean Reno) angehört und die sich auf der Jagd nach einem Koffer ihren Weg durch ein Labyrinth brutaler Actionszenen bahnen muss. / Sam (De Niro) et Vincent (Jean Reno), membres d'un groupe de mercenaires lancés à la poursuite d'une précieuse mallette dans un dédale de scènes d'action violentes.

POSTER ARTWORK FOR 'RONIN' (1998)
Veteran director John Frankenheimer said of De Niro, "What he gives is total, total believability." / Regieveteran John Frankenheimer sagte von De Niro: „Was er liefert, ist totale, totale Glaubwürdigkeit." / Réalisateur chevronné, John Frankenheimer disait de De Niro : « Ce qu'il apporte, c'est une totale crédibilité. »

"Acting is not about neurosis, playing on your neuroses. It's about the character."
Robert De Niro

„Schauspielen hat nichts mit Neurosen zu tun. Es geht nicht darum, mit seinen Neurosen zu spielen. Es geht um den Charakter."
Robert De Niro

« Le métier de comédien ne consiste pas à jouer sur ses névroses. L'important, c'est le personnage. »
Robert De Niro

STILL FROM 'RONIN' (1998)
The film is a series of gunfights and car chases that take place all over France. / Der Film besteht aus einer Reihe von Schießereien und Verfolgungsjagden quer durch Frankreich. / Le film est une succession de fusillades et de poursuites en voiture aux quatre coins de la France.

STILL FROM 'ANALYZE THIS' (1999)
When mobster Paul Vitti (De Niro) loses belief in his abilities, he turns to psychiatrist Dr. Ben Sobel (Billy Crystal) for help. / Als Mafioso Paul Vitti (De Niro) das Vertrauen in seine Fähigkeiten verliert, ersucht er den Psychiater Dr. Ben Sobel (Billy Crystal) um Hilfe. / Souffrant d'une perte de confiance en ses capacités, le parrain Paul Vitti (De Niro) demande l'aide d'un psychiatre, le Dr Ben Sobel (Billy Crystal).

STILL FROM 'ANALYZE THIS' (1999)
As the new millennium arrives, De Niro rediscovers the comic actor in himself, making fun of his film persona. / Noch vor Beginn des neuen Jahrtausends entdeckte De Niro den Komiker, der in ihm steckt, wieder und veralberte die Figuren, die er in ernsteren Filmen gespielt hatte. / À l'approche du nouveau millénaire, De Niro redécouvre ses talents d'acteur comique en tournant en dérision son personnage habituel.

STILL FROM 'FLAWLESS' (1999)
De Niro confronts the subject of homophobia (De Niro's
father was gay) in a nuanced performance as the
bigoted Walt Koontz, who is befriended by drag queen
Rusty (Philip Seymour Hoffman). / De Niro stellt sich
dem Thema Homophobie (De Niros Vater war
homosexuell) in einer nuancierten Schauspielleistung
als bigotter Walt Koontz, der sich mit dem Transvestiten
Rusty (Philip Seymour Hoffman) anfreundet. / De Niro
(dont le père était homosexuel) s'attaque au thème de
l'homophobie avec une interprétation toute en nuances
du très conservateur Walt Koontz, qui se lie d'amitié
avec la drag-queen Rusty (Philip Seymour Hoffman).

STILL FROM 'THE ADVENTURES OF ROCKY AND BULLWINKLE' (2000)
More mugging and comic antics for De Niro as the Fearless Leader, here tied up by Rocky with Natasha (Rene Russo) and Boris (Jason Alexander). / Noch mehr Grimassen und alberne Possen steckten für De Niro in der Rolle des „Furchtlosen", den Eichhörnchen Rocky hier mit den Bösewichten Natasha (Rene Russo) und Boris (Jason Alexander) zusammengeschnürt hat. / Nouvelle avalanche de grimaces et de bouffonneries dans le rôle de Fearless Leader, ligoté par Rocky aux côtés de Natasha (Rene Russo) et de Boris (Jason Alexander).

STILL FROM 'MEN OF HONOR' (2000)
De Niro found playing the racist navy instructor "Billy"
Sunday "uncomfortable" but said, "If I didn't do it
as fully as it should be done, there'd be no point in
doing it." / De Niro fühlte sich unwohl, als er hier den
rassistischen Marineausbilder „Billy" Sunday spielen
sollte, meinte aber: „Wenn ich es nicht so vollständig
getan hätte, wie es getan werden musste, dann wäre es
sinnlos gewesen, es überhaupt zu tun." / Bien qu'il se
sente « mal à l'aise » dans le rôle de « Billy » Sunday,
instructeur raciste de la Navy, De Niro déclare : « Si je
ne me donnais pas à fond, ce ne serait pas la peine de
le faire. »

STILL FROM 'MEET THE PARENTS' (2000)
De Niro scores another huge hit as a comic actor as
Jack Byrnes, the formidable and overprotective father,
subjecting his son-in-law Gaylord Focker (Ben Stiller)
to the polygraph. / De Niro landete einen weiteren
Megahit als Komiker in der Rolle von Jack Byrnes, dem
übermäßig fürsorglichen Brautvater, der seinen
künftigen Schwiegersohn Gaylord Focker (Ben Stiller)
einem Lügendetektortest unterzieht. / Encore un
immense succès comique dans le rôle de Jack Byrnes,
père redoutable et hyperprotecteur, qui soumet son
gendre Gaylord Focker (Ben Stiller) au détecteur de
mensonges.

STILL FROM '15 MINUTES' (2001)
Detective Eddie Flemming (De Niro) and fire marshal
Jordy Warsaw (Edward Burns) are two incorruptible
New York civil servants. / Kriminalpolizist Eddie
Flemming (De Niro) und Brandstiftungsexperte Jordy
Warsaw (Edward Burns) sind zwei unbestechliche
New Yorker Beamte. / L'inspecteur Eddie Flemming
(De Niro) et l'enquêteur de la brigade des incendies
criminels Jordy Warsaw (Edward Burns), deux
fonctionnaires incorruptibles de la ville de New York.

*"Some people say, 'New York's a great place to
visit, but I wouldn't want to live there.' I say that
about other places."*
Robert De Niro

*„Manche Leute sagen: ‚New York ist toll für einen
Urlaub, aber leben möchte ich dort nicht.' Ich sage
das von anderen Orten."*
Robert De Niro

*« Certains disent que New York est un endroit
génial à visiter, mais qu'ils n'aimeraient pas y vivre.
Moi, je dis ça des autres endroits. »*
Robert De Niro

STILL FROM '15 MINUTES' (2001)
Two Eastern European criminals videotape their
murders and try to sell the video to an exploitative
TV show so that they can get away with murder. Media-
savvy Eddie Flemming tries to track them down. / Zwei
osteuropäische Verbrecher zeichnen ihre Morde auf
und versuchen, das Videoband an ein ausbeuterisches
Fernsehmagazin zu verkaufen, um sich ihrer Strafe zu
entziehen. Gejagt werden sie von dem medienerprobten
Eddie Flemming. / Deux criminels d'Europe de l'Est
filment leurs meurtres et tentent de les vendre à une
émission de télévision afin d'échapper à la justice.
Fin connaisseur des médias, Eddie Flemming se lance
à leur poursuite.

STILL FROM 'THE SCORE' (2001)
Top thief Nick Wells (De Niro) is trying to retire, but his associate Max (Marlon Brando) persuades him to do one last score. Their inside man is loose cannon Jackie Teller (Edward Norton). / Meisterdieb Nick Wells (De Niro) möchte sich zur Ruhe setzen, doch sein Partner Max (Marlon Brando) überredet ihn zu einem letzten Beutezug. Als Spitzel dient ihnen der unberechenbare Jackie Teller (Edward Norton). / Alors que l'as du cambriolage Nick Wells (De Niro) s'apprête à prendre sa retraite, son associé Max (Marlon Brando) le persuade d'entreprendre un dernier coup. Hélas, leur complice Jackie Teller (Edward Norton) s'avère être un franc-tireur.

"An actor is sensitive as it is—shy—and the whole point of you doing this [acting] is that you want to express yourself. There's a kind of thread there as to why people become actors."
Robert De Niro

„Ein Schauspieler ist ohnehin schon empfindsam, schüchtern – und der Grund, weshalb man das [Schauspielen] überhaupt macht, ist, dass man sich ausdrücken möchte. Es gibt da eine Art Zusammenhang, weshalb Menschen Schauspieler werden."
Robert De Niro

STILL FROM 'THE SCORE' (2001)
In this tale of aging thieves and daring heists, nobody knows who to trust or who is going to double-cross them. / In dieser Geschichte von alternden Dieben und waghalsigen Diebstählen weiß niemand, wem er über den Weg trauen kann und wer ihn übers Ohr hauen wird. / Dans cette histoire où des cambrioleurs vieillissants entreprennent un coup risqué, personne ne sait sur qui compter ni de qui se méfier.

« Un acteur est quelqu'un de sensible, de timide, et tout l'intérêt de ce métier, c'est de pouvoir s'exprimer. Cela explique peut-être pourquoi on devient acteur. »
Robert De Niro

STILL FROM 'SHOWTIME' (2002)
In a satire on the media phenomena of "reality" shows, De Niro plays straight-down-the-line, old-fashioned LAPD cop Mitch Preston. / In einer Satire über das Medienphänomen der Realityshows spielt De Niro den altmodischen, vorschriftstreuen Polizeibeamten Mitch Preston vom Los Angeles Police Department. / Dans cette satire du phénomène médiatique de la télé-réalité, De Niro incarne Mitch Preston, un lieutenant aguerri et bourru de la police de Los Angeles.

"I've never been one of those actors who has touted myself as a fascinating human being. I had to decide early on whether I was to be an actor or a personality."
Robert De Niro

„Ich gehörte nie zu diesen Schauspielern, die sich selbst als faszinierende Menschen anpreisen. Ich musste mich früh entscheiden, ob ich Schauspieler werden wollte oder eine Persönlichkeit."
Robert De Niro

« Je n'ai jamais été de ces acteurs qui se vantent d'être des gens fascinants. J'ai dû choisir très tôt entre être un acteur et être une personnalité. »
Robert De Niro

STILL FROM 'SHOWTIME' (2002)
Preston is forced by his superiors to appear on a cop
reality show with patrol officer/wannabe actor Sellars
(Eddie Murphy). / Preston wird von seinen Vorgesetzten
genötigt, mit dem Streifenpolizisten und
Möchtegernschauspieler Sellars (Eddie Murphy) in einer
Realityshow über die Arbeit der Polizei mitzuwirken. /
Preston est contraint par ses supérieurs de passer dans
une émission de télé-réalité en compagnie de l'agent
Sellars (Eddie Murphy), qui rêve de devenir acteur.

STILL FROM 'CITY BY THE SEA' (2002)
An older De Niro, again alienated and tortured on the
streets of his beloved New York City, strikes a pose
reminiscent of 'Taxi Driver.' / Ein älterer De Niro, wieder
entfremdet und gequält in den Straßen seines geliebten
New York City und in einer Pose, die an *Taxi Driver*
erinnert. / Planté dans les rues de New York, De Niro,
malgré son âge, n'est pas sans rappeler le héros de
Taxi Driver avec son air absent et torturé.

STILL FROM 'CITY BY THE SEA' (2002)
In 'City by the Sea', based on a true story, cop Vincent
LaMarca (De Niro) investigates a murder only to find
that his alienated son Joey (James Franco) is the prime
suspect. / In *City by the Sea*, das auf einer wahren
Geschichte basiert, ermittelt der Polizist Vincent
LaMarca (De Niro) in einem Mordfall und muss dabei
feststellen, dass sein entfremdeter Sohn Joey (James
Franco) der Hauptverdächtige ist. / Inspiré d'un fait réel,
Père et flic raconte l'histoire d'un policier, Vincent
LaMarca (De Niro) qui découvre que le principal
suspect du meurtre sur lequel il enquête n'est autre
que son fils Joey (James Franco).

"When you make a drama, you spend all day beating a guy to death with a hammer, or what have you. Or, you have to take a bite out of somebody's face. On the other hand, with a comedy, you yell at Billy Crystal for an hour, and you go home."
Robert De Niro

„Wenn du ein Drama drehst, dann verbringst du den ganzen Tag damit, einen Typen mit einem Hammer - oder was auch immer - totzuschlagen. Oder du beißt jemandem ein Stück Fleisch aus dem Gesicht. Andererseits, bei einer Komödie schreit man eine Stunde lang Billy Crystal an und geht nach Hause."
Robert De Niro

« Quand on tourne un drame, on passe la journée à achever un type à coups de marteau, ou à lui arracher un bout de visage avec les dents. Quand on tourne une comédie, on hurle sur Billy Crystal pendant une heure et on rentre chez soi. »
Robert De Niro

STILL FROM 'ANALYZE THAT' (2002)
Paul Vitti (De Niro) belts out a song for his fellow inmates. / Paul Vitti (De Niro) schmettert ein Lied für seine Mitgefangenen. / Paul Vitti (De Niro) chante à pleins poumons pour ses codétenus.

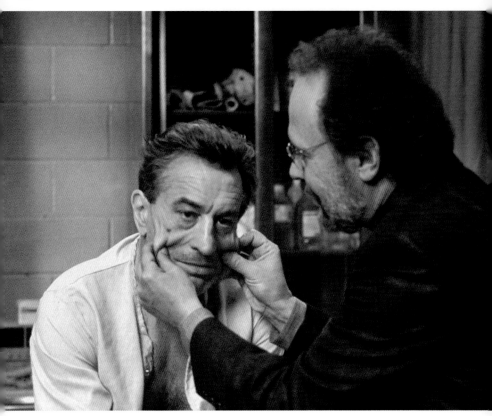

STILL FROM 'ANALYZE THAT' (2002)
In this sequel to the successful 'Analyze This,'
psychiatrist Dr. Sobel (Billy Crystal) again tries to help
the conflicted but crafty don. / In dieser Fortsetzung
der Erfolgskomödie *Reine Nervensache* versucht
Psychiater Dr. Sobel (Billy Crystal) auch wieder, dem
ebenso konfliktbelasteten wie gewieften Mafiaboss
zu helfen. / Dans la suite du célèbre *Mafia Blues*,
le Dr Sobel (Billy Crystal) tente une nouvelle
psychothérapie sur le parrain perturbé mais roublard.

STILL FROM 'ANALYZE THAT' (2002)
De Niro commits fully to his comic renditions of hits
from 'West Side Story,' here seen with Joe Viterelli as
Jelly. / De Niro geht voll und ganz in seinen witzigen
Interpretationen bekannter Nummern aus *West Side
Story* auf – hier im Bild mit Joe Viterelli als Jelly. /
De Niro s'égosille sans complexe sur les grands airs de
West Side Story, avec Joe Viterelli dans le rôle de Jelly.

STILL FROM 'GODSEND' (2004)
Dr. Richard Wells (De Niro) aids in the cloning of a child
(Cameron Bright) for a bereaved couple. / Dr. Richard
Wells (De Niro) hilft beim Klonen eines Kindes (Cameron
Bright) für ein trauerndes Ehepaar. / Le Dr Richard
Wells (De Niro) participe au clonage d'un petit garçon
(Cameron Bright) mort accidentellement.

STILL FROM 'SHARK TALE' (2004)
De Niro voiced the cartoon character Don Lino (left).
Another wiseguy, Martin Scorsese, also joined the cast. /
De Niro lieh der animierten Figur des Don Lino (links)
im Original des Films seine Stimme. Mit von der Partie
war auch sein alter „Komplize" Martin Scorsese. /
De Niro prête sa voix au personnage de Don Lino
(à gauche) dans ce film d'animation où l'on entend
également son vieux complice Martin Scorsese.

STILL FROM 'MEET THE FOCKERS' (2004)
Another sequel to an astoundingly successful film.
De Niro reprises his role as frightening father Jack
Byrnes, here overpowered by the equally intimidating
Mrs. Focker (Barbra Streisand). / Eine weitere Fort-
setzung eines erstaunlich erfolgreichen Films:
De Niro schlüpft noch einmal in die Rolle des furcht-
einflößenden Vaters Jack Byrnes, der hier von der
gleichermaßen beängstigenden Mrs. Focker (Barbra
Streisand) „in die Mangel" genommen wird. / Dans la
suite de son incroyable succès, De Niro retrouve le rôle
du terrifiant beau-père Jack Byrnes, ici dominé par une
Mme Focker tout aussi intimidante (Barbra Streisand).

STILL FROM 'MEET THE FOCKERS' (2004)
Two icons opposite each other in a bit of comic
trivia—Dustin Hoffman as the emotionally expansive
Mr. Focker. / Zwei Filmikonen in einer etwas belanglosen
Komödie: Dustin Hoffman spielt den sehr gefühls-
betonten Mr. Focker. / Deux monstres sacrés réunis
dans une scène de comédie burlesque où Dustin
Hoffman incarne le très envahissant M. Focker.

STILL FROM 'HIDE AND SEEK' (2005)
As a man dealing with the death of his wife as well as the psychological disturbances of his young daughter, De Niro delivers a powerful performance. / Als Mann, der sowohl den Tod seiner Frau als auch die psychischen Störungen seiner kleinen Tochter verkraften muss, liefert De Niro eine starke schauspielerische Leistung. / De Niro interprète avec brio le rôle d'un homme confronté à la mort de sa femme et aux troubles psychiques de sa petite fille.

STILL FROM 'THE BRIDGE OF SAN LUIS REY' (2004)
De Niro in a relatively small part as the archbishop of Peru, in an adaptation of Thornton Wilder's classic novel. / De Niro in einer verhältnismäßig kleinen Rolle als Erzbischof von Peru in einer Verfilmung des Romanklassikers von Thornton Wilder. / De Niro joue le rôle relativement modeste de l'archevêque du Pérou dans cette adaptation du roman de Thornton Wilder.

**STILL FROM 'ARTHUR AND THE INVISIBLES'
(2006)**
The King (right) was voiced by Robert De Niro in
Luc Besson's animated epic. / In der englischen
Sprachfassung dieses französischen Animationsfilms
von Luc Besson lieh Robert De Niro dem König (rechts)
seine Stimme. / Robert De Niro prête sa voix au Roi
(à droite) dans le film d'animation de Luc Besson.

STILL FROM 'THE GOOD SHEPHERD' (2006)
De Niro directs his own *Godfather* in this epic film of
the CIA, personal corruption, and tortured family
relationships starring Angelina Jolie and Matt Damon. /
De Niro dreht seinen eigenen „*Paten*", ein Filmepos
über die CIA, menschliche Verderbtheit und qualvolle
Familienverhältnisse – mit Angelina Jolie und Matt
Damon in den Hauptrollen. / De Niro tourne son propre
Parrain, une sombre histoire de CIA, de corruption et
de déchirements familiaux, avec Angelina Jolie et Matt
Damon.

*"When I'm directing a great dramatic scene, part
of me is saying, 'Thank God I don't have to do that.'
Because I know how hard it is to act. It's the middle
of the night. It's freezing. You gotta do this scene.
You gotta get it up to get to that point. And yet, as
a director, you've got to get the actors to that
point. It's hard either way."*
Robert De Niro

*„Wenn ich bei einer großen dramatischen
Szene Regie führe, dann sagt ein Teil von mir:
‚Gott sei Dank muss ich das nicht machen.' Weil
Schauspielen nämlich schwer ist, wissen Sie. Es ist
mitten in der Nacht. Es ist eiskalt. Du musst diese
Szene jetzt drehen. Du musst dich aufraffen, um an
diesen Punkt zu kommen. Aber als Regisseur muss
man die Schauspieler an diesen Punkt bringen.
Es ist so oder so schwierig."*
Robert De Niro

STILL FROM 'THE GOOD SHEPHERD' (2006)
The director takes a small but crucial role as the CIA's
first director, Bill Sullivan, who welcomes his recruit
Edward Wilson (Matt Damon) aboard. / Der Regisseur
spielt eine kleine, aber wichtige Rolle als Bill Sullivan,
der erste Direktor der CIA, der hier seinen Rekruten
Edward Wilson (Matt Damon) in der Herde willkommen
heißt. / Le réalisateur joue le rôle discret mais crucial de
Bill Sullivan, le premier directeur de la CIA, qui accueille
ici sa nouvelle recrue, Edward Wilson (Matt Damon).

*« Quand je dirige une grande scène dramatique,
je me dis au fond de moi : "Dieu merci, ce n'est pas
à moi de la jouer." Car je sais à quel point il est dur
d'être acteur. C'est le milieu de la nuit. Il fait un
froid de canard. Il faut jouer la scène. Il faut se
bouger le c... pour trouver le ton juste. À l'inverse,
en tant que réalisateur, il faut aider les acteurs à
trouver le ton juste. C'est dur dans les deux cas. »*
Robert De Niro

PAGES 168/169
STILL FROM 'THE GOOD SHEPHERD' (2006)
De Niro shows both a visual flair, much like his mentor
Scorsese, as well as a subtlety when directing the
actors. / De Niro beweist sowohl seinen Instinkt für das
Visuelle – ganz wie sein Mentor Scorsese – als auch ein
gutes Händchen im Umgang mit den Schauspielern. /
De Niro fait preuve d'un sens visuel qui n'est pas sans
rappeler celui de son mentor, Scorsese, ainsi que d'une
grande finesse dans la direction d'acteurs.

**ON THE SET OF 'THE GOOD SHEPHERD'
(2006)**
De Niro with screenwriter Eric Roth, with whom he
nurtured this project for many years. / De Niro mit
Drehbuchautor Eric Roth, mit dem er dieses Projekt
über viele Jahre hinweg plante. / De Niro et le
scénariste Eric Roth, avec lequel il a nourri ce projet
pendant de nombreuses années.

STILL FROM 'THE GOOD SHEPHERD' (2006)
Edward Wilson shuts out all emotion in his life,
including his wife, Margaret (Angelina Jolie). / Edward
Wilson blendet alle Gefühle aus seinem Leben aus –
auch gegenüber seiner Ehefrau Margaret (Angelina
Jolie). / Edward Wilson est fermé à toute forme
d'émotion, y compris à l'égard de sa femme, Margaret
(Angelina Jolie).

STILL FROM 'STARDUST' (2007)
Captain Shakespeare (De Niro), the pirate with a
fearsome reputation, shows some of the lightning he
has captured in this whimsical fantasy. / Captain
Shakespeare (De Niro), der als furchterregend
verschriene Pirat, zeigt in diesem skurrilen Märchen
einige der Blitze, die er eingefangen hat. / Le capitaine
Shakespeare (De Niro), pirate à la terrible réputation,
brandit la foudre qu'il a capturée dans ce conte
fantastique.

"Everybody wants De Niro. He hasn't had many
hits but he represents quality and integrity."
Brian Grazer, producer

„Jeder will De Niro haben. Er hat nicht viele
Kassenschlager gehabt, aber er steht für Qualität
und Integrität."
Brian Grazer, Produzent

« Tout le monde veut De Niro. Il n'a pas eu
beaucoup de très gros succès, mais il est
synonyme de qualité et d'intégrité. »
Brian Grazer, producteur

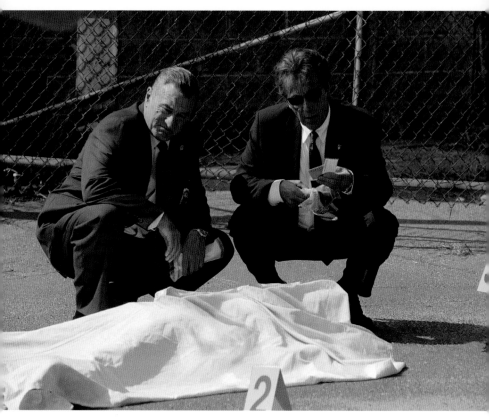

STILL FROM 'RIGHTEOUS KILL' (2008)
Turk (De Niro) and Rooster (Pacino) play cops trying
to find a serial killer who is murdering criminals. / Turk
(De Niro) und Rooster (Pacino) spielen Polizisten, die
versuchen, einen Serienmörder dingfest zu machen,
der Verbrecher umbringt. / Turk (De Niro) et Rooster
(Pacino), deux flics sur la trace d'un serial killer qui
assassine des criminels.

STILL FROM 'RIGHTEOUS KILL' (2008)
They want to pin a medal on the killer rather than put
him in jail. But all the evidence is starting to point to
Turk as the killer. / Sie wollen dem Mörder lieber einen
Orden verleihen, statt ihn ins Gefängnis zu stecken.
Allerdings beginnen alle Indizien darauf hinzudeuten,
dass in Wahrheit Turk der Mörder ist. / Alors qu'ils
aimeraient mieux décerner une médaille au tueur que
de le jeter en prison, tous les indices commencent à
pointer en direction de Turk.

PAGES 176/177
STILL FROM 'WHAT JUST HAPPENED?' (2008)
In a critique of Hollywood, based on Art Linson's
memoir, De Niro plays a troubled producer for director
Barry Levinson. / In einer Hollywood-Kritik nach den
Memoiren von Art Linson spielt De Niro unter der
Regie von Barry Levinson einen sorgengeplagten
Filmproduzenten. / De Niro en producteur tourmenté
dans une critique d'Hollywood inspirée des mémoires
d'Art Linson et mise en scène par Barry Levinson.

PAGE 178
**ON THE SET OF 'THE GOOD SHEPHERD'
(2006)**
De Niro can now claim a place as an accomplished
director as well as an iconic actor. / De Niro hat sich
nicht nur als Schauspielikone, sondern auch als
talentierter Regisseur einen Namen gemacht. / Non
content d'être un acteur de légende, De Niro est
désormais reconnu comme un réalisateur accompli.

3
CHRONOLOGY

CHRONOLOGIE

CHRONOLOGIE

CHRONOLOGY

17 August 1943 Robert Mario De Niro Jr. is born in New York City to artists Robert De Niro and Virginia Admiral.

1959–1963 Tours in a production of Chekhov's *The Bear* and appears in other plays. Attends Stella Adler Conservatory and Lee Strasberg's Actors Studio.

1963 Appears in *The Wedding Party* (not released until 1969), codirected by Brian De Palma.

1968 Stars in De Palma's film *Greetings*.

1970 Stars in De Palma's *Hi, Mom!*

1973 First real critical recognition for his role as a dying baseball player in *Bang the Drum Slowly* and as Johnny Boy in Martin Scorsese's *Mean Streets*. Begins a decades-long creative relationship with Scorsese.

1974 Wins Academy Award for his role as the young Vito Corleone in Francis Ford Coppola's *The Godfather: Part II*.

1976 Marries model/actress Diahnne Abbott (divorced 1988). Academy Award nomination for his role as Travis Bickle in *Taxi Driver*.

1977 Reunites with Scorsese for musical drama *New York, New York*, costarring Liza Minnelli.

1978 Nominated for Academy Award for his role in the controversial Vietnam war film *The Deer Hunter*.

1980 Gains weight for role as boxer Jake La Motta in Scorsese's *Raging Bull*; wins another Academy Award.

1982 Close friend comedian John Belushi dies of a drug overdose at the Chateau Marmont; De Niro is briefly questioned about the case.

1983 Plays delusional comedian Rupert Pupkin in Scorsese's *The King of Comedy*.

1986 Takes on the physically demanding role of slaver-turned-priest Rodrigo Mendoza in Roland Joffé's epic *The Mission*.

1988 Expands his acting range to include straight comedic roles with *Midnight Run*.

1989 Begins investing in the Tribeca neighborhood of New York City; bases his film company and restaurant there.

1990 Nominated for an Academy Award for his role as the semicatatonic patient in *Awakenings*; plays a supporting role in Scorsese's *GoodFellas*.

1993 Directs his first film, *A Bronx Tale*. De Niro's father dies of cancer.

1995 For the first time De Niro appears opposite fellow New York "method" actor Al Pacino in Michael Mann's *Heat*. With Scorsese by his side he takes on the Vegas Mob in *Casino*.

1997 Marries flight attendant Grace Hightower.

1999 Returns to comedy in the financially successful *Analyze This* with Billy Crystal.

2000 Stars in another comedic hit: *Meet the Parents*.

2002 Appears in and narrates the documentary *9/11*.

2003 Diagnosed and treated for prostate cancer.

2006 Italy confers honorary citizenship on De Niro. Directs *The Good Shepherd*, a critique of the CIA.

PORTRAIT FOR 'ANALYZE THAT' (2002)

CHRONOLOGIE

17. August 1943 Robert Mario De Niro jr. wird in New York City als Sohn der Künstler Robert De Niro und Virginia Admiral geboren.

1959–1963 Er geht mit einer Aufführung von Tschechows Einakter *Der Bär* auf Theatertournee und tritt auch in anderen Stücken auf. Er besucht das Stella Adler Conservatory sowie Lee Strasbergs Actors Studio.

1963 Er steht in dem Film *The Wedding Party*, der erst 1969 in die Kinos kommt, vor der Kamera. Brian De Palma ist einer der Regisseure.

1968 Spielt die Hauptrolle in De Palmas Film *Greetings – Grüße*.

1970 Spielt die Hauptrolle in De Palmas Film *Hi, Mom!*.

1973 Erfährt erste wirkliche Anerkennung durch die Kritiker für seine Darstellung eines sterbenden Baseballspielers in *Das letzte Spiel* und als Johnny Boy in Martin Scorseses *Hexenkessel*, mit dem eine jahrzehntelange berufliche Beziehung zu Scorsese beginnt.

1974 Erhält einen Academy Award („Oscar") für seine Rolle als junger Vito Corleone in Francis Ford Coppolas *Der Pate: Teil II*.

1976 Heiratet Model/Schauspielerin Diahnne Abbott (Scheidung 1988). Academy-Award-Nominierung für seine Rolle als Travis Bickle in *Taxi Driver*.

1977 Spielt wieder unter Scorseses Regie in dem Musical-Drama *New York, New York* mit Liza Minnelli in der weiblichen Hauptrolle.

1978 Wird für einen Academy Award nominiert für seine Rolle in dem umstrittenen Vietnam-kriegsfilm *Die durch die Hölle gehen*.

1980 Nimmt für seine Rolle als Boxer Jake La Motta in Scorseses *Wie ein wilder Stier* an Gewicht zu; gewinnt einen weiteren Academy Award.

PORTRAIT FOR 'NEW YORK, NEW YORK'
(1977)

1982 Sein enger Freund John Belushi stirbt an einer Überdosis Drogen im Chateau Marmont Hotel; De Niro wird zu diesem Fall kurz verhört.

1983 Spielt den obsessiven Komiker Rupert Pupkin in Scorseses *King of Comedy*.

1986 Übernimmt die körperlich anstrengende Rolle des vom Sklavenhalter zum Priester gewandelten Rodrigo Mendoza in Roland Joffés *Mission*.

1988 Erweitert sein schauspielerisches Repertoire durch reine Comedy-Rollen wie in *Midnight Run – 5 Tage bis Mitternacht*.

1989 Beginnt seine Investitionen in den New Yorker Stadtteil Tribeca, indem er hier seine Film-produktionsfirma und sein Restaurant ansiedelt.

1990 Wird für seine Rolle als Schlafkranker in *Zeit des Erwachens* für einen Academy Award nominiert; spielt eine Nebenrolle in Scorseses *GoodFellas – Drei Jahrzehnte in der Mafia*.

1993 Führt erstmals selbst Regie: *In den Straßen der Bronx*. De Niros Vater stirbt an Krebs.

1995 De Niro steht in Michael Manns *Heat* erstmals mit seinem New Yorker Schauspiel- und Method-Acting-Kollegen Al Pacino vor der Kamera. Mit Scorsese als Regisseur nimmt es er es in *Casino* mit der Mafia von Las Vegas auf.

1997 Heiratet die Flugbegleiterin Grace Hightower.

1999 Kehrt mit dem kommerziell erfolgreichen Film *Reine Nervensache* zur Komödie zurück.

2000 Spielt eine Hauptrolle in einer weiteren Hit-Komödie: *Meine Braut, ihr Vater und ich*.

2002 Steht in der amerikanischen Fassung des französischen Fernsehfilms *9/11* vor der Kamera und spricht auch den Kommentar.

2003 Bei ihm wird Prostatakrebs diagnostiziert und behandelt.

2006 Italien verleiht De Niro die Ehrenstaats-bürgerschaft. Er führt Regie bei *Der gute Hirte*, einer Kritik an der CIA.

CHRONOLOGIE

17 août 1943 Naissance à New York de Robert Mario De Niro Jr., fils des artistes Robert De Niro et Virginia Admiral.

1959–1963 Joue dans *L'Ours* de Tchekhov et apparaît dans d'autres pièces. Étudie au Conservatoire de Stella Adler et à l'Actors Studio de Lee Strasberg.

1963 Apparaît dans *Le Mariage* (sorti en 1969), coréalisé par Brian De Palma.

1968 Décroche le premier rôle dans *Greetings* de Brian De Palma.

1970 Occupe le premier rôle dans *Hi, Mom!* de Brian De Palma.

1973 Première véritable reconnaissance critique pour son rôle de joueur de base-ball mourant dans *Le Dernier Match* et pour celui de Johnny Boy dans *Mean Streets* de Martin Scorsese. Entame une collaboration de plusieurs décennies avec Scorsese.

1974 Remporte l'oscar du Meilleur acteur pour le rôle du jeune Vito Corleone dans *Le Parrain 2* de Francis Ford Coppola.

1976 Épouse l'actrice et mannequin Diahnne Abbott (divorce en 1988). Sélectionné aux Oscars pour le rôle de Travis Bickle dans *Taxi Driver*.

1977 Retrouve Scorsese dans le film musical *New York, New York* avec Liza Minnelli.

1978 Sélectionné aux Oscars pour son rôle dans *Voyage au bout de l'enfer*, film controversé sur la guerre du Vietnam.

1980 Interprète le rôle du boxeur Jake La Motta dans *Raging Bull* de Scorsese, pour lequel il prend 30 kilos et remporte un nouvel oscar.

1982 Est brièvement interrogé par la police suite au décès de son ami, le comédien John Belushi, mort d'une overdose au Château Marmont.

1983 Joue le rôle d'un humoriste prêt à tout pour réussir dans *La Valse des pantins* de Scorsese.

1986 Interprète le rôle très physique d'un marchand d'esclaves repenti dans *Mission*, film épique de Roland Joffé.

1988 Élargit son répertoire en se lançant dans la comédie pure avec *Midnight Run*.

1989 Commence à investir dans le quartier de Tribeca, à New York, où il ouvre une société de production et un restaurant.

1990 Sélectionné aux Oscars pour son rôle de patient léthargique dans *L'Éveil*. Interprète un second rôle dans *Les Affranchis* de Scorsese.

1993 Réalise son premier film, *Il était une fois le Bronx*. Son père meurt d'un cancer.

1995 Dans *Heat* de Michael Mann, il joue pour la première fois avec Al Pacino, son ancien camarade de l'Actors Studio. Dans *Casino* de Scorsese, il incarne un chef de la mafia de Las Vegas.

1997 Épouse l'hôtesse de l'air Grace Hightower.

1999 Revient à la comédie avec le succès commercial *Mafia blues*, avec Billy Crystal.

2000 Est la vedette d'une autre comédie à succès : *Mon beau-père et moi*.

2002 Apparaît dans le documentaire *11/09, New York 11 septembre*.

2003 Se voit diagnostiquer un cancer de la prostate, pour lequel il est traité.

2006 Reçoit la nationalité italienne à titre honorifique. Réalise *Raisons d'État*, critique de la CIA.

PORTRAIT FOR 'ANALYZE THAT' (2002)

COLUMBIA PICTURES presents

ROBERT DE NIRO

TAXI DRIVER

A BILL/PHILLIPS Production of a MARTIN SCORSESE Film

JODIE FOSTER | ALBERT BROOKS as "Tom" HARVEY KEITEL

LEONARD HARRIS | PETER BOYLE as "Wizard" | and

CYBILL SHEPHERD as "Betsy"

Written by PAUL SCHRADER Music BERNARD HERRMANN Produced by MICHAEL PHILLIPS

and JULIA PHILLIPS Directed by MARTIN SCORSESE Production Services by Devon/Persky·Bright

R RESTRICTED

4

FILMOGRAPHY

FILMOGRAFIE

FILMOGRAPHIE

The Wedding Party (1963/1969)
Cecil. Directors/Regie/réalisation: Brian De Palma, Wilford Leach, Cynthia Munroe.

Trois Chambres à Manhattan (dt. *Drei Zimmer in Manhattan*, fr. *Trois chambres à Manhattan*, 1965)
Patron in Dinner/Gast beim Abendessen/un client au dîner. Director/Regie/réalisation: Marcel Carné.

Greetings (dt. *Greetings – Grüße*, 1968)
Jon Rubin. Director/Regie/réalisation: Brian De Palma.

Sam's Song (dt. *Wer die Killer ruft*, 1969)
Sam Nicoletti. Directors/Regie/réalisation: John Shade, John C. Broderick.

Bloody Mama (1970)
Lloyd Barker. Director/Regie/réalisation: Roger Corman.

Hi, Mom! (1970)
Jon Rubin. Director/Regie/réalisation: Brian De Palma.

Jennifer on My Mind (1971)
Mardigian. Director/Regie/réalisation: Noel Black.

Born to Win (dt. *Pforte zur Hölle*, fr. *Né pour vaincre*, 1971)
Danny. Director/Regie/réalisation: Ivan Passer.

The Gang That Couldn't Shoot Straight (dt. *Wo Gangster um die Ecke knallen / Spaghetti Killer*, 1971)
Mario Trantino. Director/Regie/réalisation: James Goldstone.

Bang the Drum Slowly (dt. *Das letzte Spiel*, fr. *Le Dernier Match*, 1973)
Bruce Pearson. Director/Regie/réalisation: John D. Hancock.

Mean Streets (dt. *Hexenkessel*, 1973)
John "Johnny Boy" Civello. Director/Regie/réalisation: Martin Scorsese.

The Godfather: Part II (dt. *Der Pate: Teil II*, fr. *Le Parrain 2*, 1974)
Vito Corleone. Director/Regie/réalisation: Francis Ford Coppola.

The Last Tycoon (dt. *Der letzte Tycoon*, fr. *Le Dernier Nabab*, 1976)
Monroe Stahr. Director/Regie/réalisation: Elia Kazan.

Taxi Driver (1976)
Travis Bickle. Director/Regie/réalisation: Martin Scorsese.

1900 [Novecento] (1976)
Alfredo Berlinghieri. Director/Regie/réalisation: Bernardo Bertolucci.

New York, New York (1977)
Jimmy Doyle. Director/Regie/réalisation: Martin Scorsese.

The Deer Hunter (dt. *Die durch die Hölle gehen*, fr. *Voyage au bout de l'enfer*, 1978)
Michael. Director/Regie/réalisation: Michael Cimino.

Raging Bull (dt. *Wie ein wilder Stier*, 1980)
Jake La Motta. Director/Regie/réalisation: Martin Scorsese.

True Confessions (dt. *Fesseln der Macht*, fr. *Sanglantes confessions*, 1981)
Pater Des Spellacy. Director/Regie/réalisation: Ulu Grosbard.

The King of Comedy (dt. *King of Comedy*, fr. *La Valse des pantins*, 1982)
Rupert Pupkin. Director/Regie/réalisation: Martin Scorsese.

Falling in Love (dt. *Der Liebe verfallen*, 1984)
Frank Raftis. Director/Regie/réalisation: Ulu Grosbard.

Once Upon a Time in America (dt. *Es war einmal in Amerika*, fr. *Il était une fois en Amérique*, 1984)
David "Noodles" Aaronson. Director/Regie/réalisation: Sergio Leone.

Brazil (1985)
Archibald "Harry" Tuttle. Director/Regie/réalisation: Terry Gilliam.

The Mission (dt. *Mission*, fr. *Mission*, 1986)
Rodrigo Mendoza. Director/Regie/réalisation: Roland Joffé.

Angel Heart (1987)
Louis Cyphre. Director/Regie/réalisation: Alan Parker.

The Untouchables (dt. *The Untouchables – Die Unbestechlichen*, fr. *Les Incorruptibles*, 1987)
Al Capone. Director/Regie/réalisation: Brian De Palma.

Midnight Run (dt. *Midnight Run – 5 Tage bis Mitternacht*, 1988)
Jack Walsh. Director/Regie/réalisation: Martin Brest.

Jacknife (dt. *Jacknife – Vom Leben betrogen*, 1989)
Joseph "Jacknife" Megessey. Director/Regie/réalisation: David Hugh Jones.

We're No Angels (dt. *Wir sind keine Engel*, fr. *Nous ne sommes pas des anges*, 1989)
Ned. Director/Regie/réalisation: Neil Jordan.

Stanley & Iris (dt. *Stanley und Iris*, fr. *Stanley & Iris*, 1990)
Stanley Everett Cox. Director/Regie/réalisation: Martin Ritt.

GoodFellas (dt. *GoodFellas – Drei Jahrzehnte in der Mafia*, fr. *Les Affranchis*, 1990)
Jimmy Conway. Director/Regie/réalisation: Martin Scorsese.

Awakenings (dt. *Zeit des Erwachens*, fr. *L'Éveil*, 1990)
Leonard Lowe. Director/Regie/réalisation: Penny Marshall.

Guilty by Suspicion (dt. *Schuldig bei Verdacht*, fr. *La Liste noire*, 1991)
David Merrill. Director/Regie/réalisation: Irwin Winkler.

Backdraft (dt. *Backdraft – Männer, die durchs Feuer gehen*, 1991)
Donald "Sgadow" Rimgale. Director/Regie/réalisation: Ron Howard.

Cape Fear (dt. *Kap der Angst*, fr. *Les Nerfs à vif*, 1991)
Max Cady. Director/Regie/réalisation: Martin Scorsese.

Mistress (dt. *Mistress – Die Geliebten von Hollywood*, 1992)
Evan M. Wright. Director/Regie/réalisation: Barry Primus.

Night and the City (dt. *Die Nacht von Soho*, fr. *La Loi de la nuit*, 1992)
Harry Fabian. Director/Regie/réalisation: Irwin Winkler.

Mad Dog and Glory (dt. *Sein Name ist Mad Dog*, 1993)
Wayne "Mad Dog" Dobie. Director/Regie/réalisation: John McNaughton.

This Boy's Life (dt. *This Boy's Life - Die Geschichte einer Jugend*, fr. *Blessures secrètes*, 1993)
Dwight Hansen. Director/Regie/réalisation: Michael Caton-Jones.

A Bronx Tale (dt. *In den Straßen der Bronx*, fr. *Il était une fois le Bronx*, 1993)
Lorenzo Anello. Director/Regie/réalisation: Robert De Niro.

Mary Shelley's Frankenstein (fr. *Frankenstein*, 1994)
The Creature/Die Kreatur/la Créature. Director/Regie/réalisation: Kenneth Branagh.

Les Cent et une Nuits de Simon Cinéma (dt. *101 Nacht - Die Träume des M. Cinéma*, 1995)
Cameo/Cameo-Auftritt/brève apparition. Director/Regie/réalisation: Agnès Varda.

Casino (1995)
Sam "Ace" Rothstein. Director/Regie/réalisation: Martin Scorsese.

Heat (1995)
Neil McCauley. Director/Regie/réalisation: Michael Mann.

The Fan (dt. *Der Fan*, fr. *Le Fan*, 1996)
Gil Renard. Director/Regie/réalisation: Tony Scott.

Sleepers (1996)
Pater Bobby. Director/Regie/réalisation: Barry Levinson.

Marvin's Room (dt. *Marvins Töchter*, fr. *Simples secrets*, 1996)
Dr. Wally. Director/Regie/réalisation: Jerry Zaks.

Cop Land (1997)
Lieutenant Moe Tilden. Director/Regie/réalisation: James Mangold.

Wag the Dog (dt. *Wag the Dog - Wenn der Schwanz mit dem Hund wedelt*, fr. *Des hommes d'influence*, 1997)
Conrad Brean. Director/Regie/réalisation: Barry Levinson.

Jackie Brown (1997)
Louis Gara. Director/Regie/réalisation: Quentin Tarantino.

Great Expectations (dt. *Große Erwartungen*, fr. *De grandes espérances*, 1998)
Arthur Lustig. Director/Regie/réalisation: Alfonso Cuarón.

Ronin (1998)
Sam. Director/Regie/réalisation: John Frankenheimer.

Analyze This (dt. *Reine Nervensache*, fr. *Mafia blues*, 1999)
Paul Vitti. Director/Regie/réalisation: Harold Ramis.

Flawless (dt. *Makellos*, fr. *Personne n'est parfait(e)*, 1999)
Walt Koontz. Director/Regie/réalisation: Joel Schumacher.

The Adventures of Rocky and Bullwinkle (dt. *Die Abenteuer von Rocky und Bullwinkle*, fr. *Les Aventures de Rocky et Bullwinkle*, 2000)
Fearless Leader/„Der Furchtlose". Director/Regie/réalisation: Des McAnuff.

Men of Honor (fr. *Les Chemins de la dignité*, 2000)
Chief Leslie W. "Billy" Sunday. Director/Regie/réalisation: George Tillman jr.

Meet the Parents (dt. *Meine Braut, ihr Vater und ich*, fr. *Mon beau-père et moi*, 2000)
Jack Byrnes. Director/Regie/réalisation: Jay Roach.

15 Minutes (dt. *15 Minuten Ruhm*, fr. *15 minutes*, 2001)
Detective Eddie Flemming. Director/Regie/réalisation: John Herzfeld.

The Score (2001)
Nick Wells. Director/Regie/réalisation: Frank Oz.

Showtime (2002)
Detective Mitch Preston. Director/Regie/réalisation: Tom Dey.

City by the Sea (fr. *Père et flic*, 2002)
Vincent LaMarca. Director/Regie/réalisation: Michael Caton-Jones.

Analyze That (dt. *Reine Nervensache 2*, fr. *Mafia blues 2 – la rechute !*, 2002)
Paul Vitti. Director/Regie/réalisation: Harold Ramis.

Godsend (fr. *Godsend, expérience interdite*, 2004)
Richard Wells. Director/Regie/réalisation: Nick Hamm.

Shark Tale (dt. *Große Haie – kleine Fische*, fr. *Gang de requins*, 2004)
Don Lino (Voice/Stimme/voix). Director/Regie/réalisation: Bibo Bergeron.

Meet the Fockers (dt. *Meine Frau, ihre Schwiegereltern und ich*, fr. *Mon beau-père, mes parents et moi*, 2004)
Jack Byrnes. Director/Regie/réalisation: Jay Roach.

The Bridge of San Luis Rey (dt. *Die Brücke von San Luis Rey*, fr. *Le Pont du roi Saint-Louis*, 2004)
Archbishop of Peru/Erzbischof von Peru/archevêque du Pérou. Director/Regie/réalisation: Mary McGuckian.

Hide and Seek (dt. *Hide and Seek – Du kannst dich nicht verstecken*, fr. *Trouble jeu*, 2005)
David Callaway. Director/Regie/réalisation: John Polson.

Arthur and the Invisibles (dt. *Arthur und die Minimoys*, fr. *Arthur et les Minimoys*, 2006)
King/König/le roi (Voice/Stimme/voix). Director/Regie/réalisation: Luc Besson.

The Good Shepherd (dt. *Der gute Hirte*, fr. *Raisons d'État*, 2006)
General Bill Sullivan. Director/Regie/réalisation: Robert De Niro.

Stardust (dt. *Der Sternwanderer*, 2007)
Captain Shakespeare. Director/Regie/réalisation: Matthew Vaughn.

What Just Happened? (2008)
Ben. Director/Regie/réalisation: Barry Levinson.

Righteous Kill (dt. *Kurzer Prozess – Righteous Kill*, fr. *La Loi et l'ordre*, 2008)
Turk. Director/Regie/réalisation: Jon Avnet.

BIBLIOGRAPHY

Agan, Patrick: *De Niro, The Man, The Myth, and The Movies.* New York, 2001.

Baxter, John: *De Niro: A Biography.* London, 2002.

Brode, Douglas: *The Films of Robert De Niro.* New York, 1999.

Cameron-Wilson, James: *The Cinema of Robert De Niro.* London, 1986.

Cosgrove, Bill: *Robert De Niro and the Fireman.* New York, 1997.

Dougan, Andy: *Untouchable: A Biography of Robert De Niro.* New York, 1996.

Dureau, Christian: *Robert De Niro.* Paris, 2006.

Horst, Sabine (Hrsg.): *Robert De Niro.* Berlin, 2002.

McKay, Keith: *Robert De Niro: The Hero Behind the Masks.* New York, 1986.

Powell, Elfreda: *Robert De Niro.* New York, 1997.

Zurhorst, Meinolf: *Robert De Niro: Seine Filme, sein Leben.* Munich, 1987.

IMPRINT

© 2009 TASCHEN GmbH
Hohenzollernring 53, D-50 672 Köln
www.taschen.com

Editor/Picture Research/Layout: Paul Duncan/Wordsmith Solutions
Editorial Coordination: Martin Holz, Cologne
Production Coordination: Nadia Najm, Cologne
German translation: Thomas J. Kinne, Nauheim
French translation: Anne Le Bot, Paris
Multilingual production: www.arnaudbriand.com, Paris
Typeface Design: Sense/Net, Andy Disl and Birgit Eichwede, Cologne

Printed in China
ISBN: 978-3-8365-0847-6

To stay informed about upcoming TASCHEN titles, please request our magazine at www.taschen.com/magazine or write to TASCHEN, Hohenzollernring 53, D-50672 Cologne, Germany; contact@taschen.com; Fax: +49-221-254919. We will be happy to send you a free copy of our magazine, which is filled with information about all of our books.

All the photos in this book, except for those listed below, were supplied by The Kobal Collection.
Steve Schapiro: 34, 37.
Thanks to Dave Kent, Phil Moad and everybody at The Kobal Collection for their professionalism and kindness.

Copyright

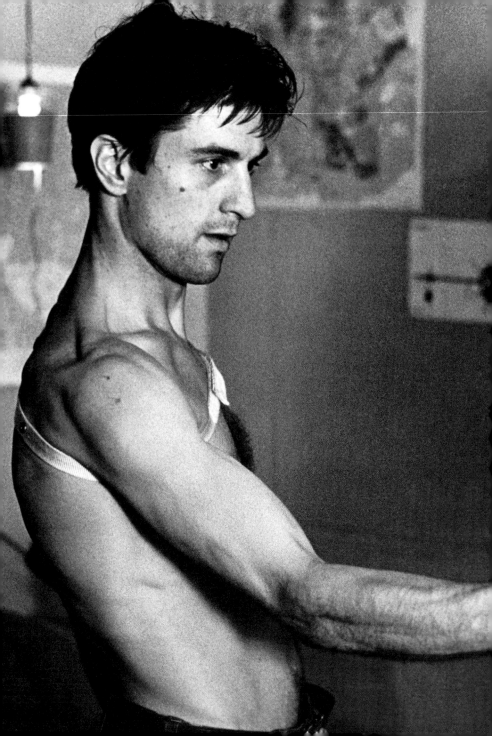